CHRISTIANS TALK ABOUT BUDDHIST MEDITATION
BUDDHISTS TALK ABOUT CHRISTIAN PRAYER

CHRISTIANS TALK ABOUT BUDDHIST MEDITATION

BUDDHISTS TALK ABOUT CHRISTIAN PRAYER

Edited by
Rita M. Gross
and
Terry C. Muck

continuum
NEW YORK • LONDON

2003

The Continuum International Publishing Group Inc
370 Lexington Avenue, New York, NY 10017

The Continuum International Publishing Group Ltd
The Tower Building, 11 York Road, London SE1 7NX

Originally published as portions of
Buddhist-Christian Studies 21 (2001) and 22 (2002)
Copyright © by University of Hawai'i Press
Introduction © 2003 by Terry C. Muck
Conclusion © 2003 by Rita M. Gross
"Buddhist Prayer?: A Reflection" © 2003 by Mahinda Deegalle

Printed in the United States of America

Library of Congress Cataloging-in-Publication Data
Christians talk about Buddhist meditation, Buddhists talk about
Christian prayer / edited by Rita M. Gross and Terry C. Muck
    p. cm.
    ISBN 0-8264-1438-9 (hardcover : alk. paper) – ISBN 0-8264-1439-7
(pbk. : alk. paper)
    1. Christianity and other religions – Buddhism. 2. Buddhism –
Relations – Christianity. 3. Prayer – Christianity. 4. Meditation –
Buddhism. I. Gross, Rita M. II. Muck, Terry C., 1947-
BR128.B8C468 2003
248.3 – dc21
                                              2003002039

Contents

Introduction

TERRY C. MUCK

Asbury Theological Seminary

This book is a collection of articles drawn from volumes 21 and 22 of *Buddhist Christian Studies,* an annual journal Rita Gross and I co-edit, published by the Society for Buddhist Christian Studies and the University of Hawai'i Press. It follows the same dialogue format that we used in volume 19 of *Buddhist-Christian Studies.* Those articles, eventually published as a book, *Buddhists Talk about the Jesus, Christians Talk about the Buddha* (Continuum, 2000), asked Christians and Buddhists to critique the founder of the other's religion. The format proved successful and provoked some good methodological discussion (see Ingram, *Buddhist Christian Studies* 21, pp. xx–xx). As we noted at the time, we think that this kind of cross-religion dialogue is the next step in interreligious interchange:

> Jesus and Gautama are important foci of their respective traditions. Thus it has always been and thus it is today. Books about Jesus have become something of a cottage industry in Christian publishing, and the visibility of the Buddha in Western academic and spirituality circles has steadily grown as the number of committed Buddhists has grown, both on a grassroots level and on the level of public figures. But we sensed that adherents of each tradition were becoming increasingly interested in the other tradition's founder. Jesus is no longer just a name to many Buddhists, but someone in whom they are very interested. To Christians, Gautama is no longer a murky creation of Herman Hesse's imagination, but a historical personage of great importance. We thought that in that interest itself lay a fruitful area of possible interreligious interchange. If Buddhists could speak candidly

of their thoughts and feelings for Jesus of Nazareth, both good thoughts/ feelings and not-so-good thoughts/feelings, the potential for learning was great. The same dynamic would apply to Christians speaking about Gautama. Commenting on the other religious tradition's founder, we thought, could provide a significant new model of interreligious dialogue. Our intuitions were on target. As the articles came in, we realized a number of things. First, we received an incredible diversity of opinion. We had intentionally left the assignment vague in terms of how the commentators would write — questions asked, style used, content covered — all these were up to the writers as they saw fit. Still, we were amazed, and frankly pleased, with the variety of views and approaches represented by the essays. Some were academic in nature, others impressionistic, some almost confessional. (*Buddhist Christian Studies* 19)

Christians Talk about Buddhist Meditation, Buddhists Talk about Christian Prayer continues the format with a new question: How have you used and/or learned from the meditative and prayer practices of the other tradition? The assignment drew enthusiastic response, especially from Christians who were asked to write about their experiences of Buddhist meditation. Frances Adeney, Mary Frohlich, Paul Ingram, Terry Muck, and Bardwell Smith (with responses by two Buddhists, Grace Burford and Robert Thurman) speak both theoretically and practically of their experiences of studying and using Buddhist meditation. Five Buddhist authors, Robert Aitken, Mahinda Deegalle, Rita Gross, Kenneth Tanaka, and Taitetsu Unno (with two Christian respondents, Ursula King and Donald Mitchell), did the same in regard to Christian prayer, albeit with less enthusiasm. In general it is fair to say that the Christians were more eager to take on this assignment than were Buddhists. In the conclusion to the book, Rita Gross reflects on why she thinks this was so.

In case you may have some ideas about why this might have happened, let us give you the facts of the case, so you can, as Agatha Cristie's Hercule Poirot was often found of saying, "exercise the little gray cells" of the brain in an informed way.

First, who we are. Rita Gross and Terry Muck are both academics and practitioners, both scholars of religion and members of specific religious traditions. We don't pretend that these two roles can be entirely separated but rather that the best way to function as scholars practitioners is to be candid about who we are and what we believe. Of course, we acknowledge that as scholars we are called upon to be objective, even-handed, and fair in our assessments of all religions, but since those traits (reflecting commitments to truth, love, and justice) are also part of each of our religious tradition's beliefs, we do not see them as in any way antithetical to our roles as practitioners of religion. The fact that some people in each of our traditions do not live up to the ideals of those traditions should not, in our judgment, cause us (or anyone else) to despair of trying to live up to them ourselves. Or to force us unnaturally to closet those commitments in our public life.

To be more specific, Rita Gross is a practicing Buddhist and Terry Muck is a practicing Christian. As editors of a journal devoted to publishing articles about the various interactions between and among adherents of Buddhism and Christianity, we see our interaction as co-editors to be a microcosm of the journal itself. We find that the partnership works, and in some measure we see that as a sign that interreligious interactions of the sort we describe in our journal work. We do not think it is because we are, either of us, that much different from most Buddhists and Christians. We are not part-time religionists. We don't, either of us, think that all religions are the same. Neither of us believes that our religious commitments are optional, fashionable, or inconsequential. We are what we are because we believe that our religion reflects truth. Yet we have never, in five years of working together, had to come to a place in our editorial duties where we could not agree on what had to be done.

Second, what we did. To illustrate, let's use the process we went through in producing the articles published in this book. We meet every summer to plan the following year's issue of *Buddhist Christian Studies.* Rita lives in Eau Claire, Wisconsin, and Terry has a summer home near Mercer, Wisconsin. In the summer of 1999 we met at Rita's house and decided to do a set of articles on spiritual practice, and we thought that the subject fit the format we are using in this book. We began to brainstorm names of authors who could write on this subject. We developed a list of about twenty Buddhists and Christians and then worked from that to try and get a spread of representatives of the various sectors of each tradition. The assignment simply asked the question: What have you, as a Buddhist (or Christian), learned from the spiritual practices of Christianity (or Buddhism)? Tell us in three thousand words.

About half the people we contacted said yes to the assignment. Two or three more wanted additional information. We still had our longer list, and to replace those who could not do the assignment because of time pressures or lack of interest, we simply went down the list and tapped other names. As we implied earlier, more Buddhists than Christians turned down the assignment, and in her conclusion Rita speculates on why that was so.

Finally, what we learned. In doing this collection of articles, we made three observations related to good interreligious interchanges. The first is that this form of dialogue requires a good deal of trust among the participants. Talking candidly about important features of the other person's religion runs the risk of offense. Yet the way the writers and respondents — mostly longtime members of the Society for Buddhist Christian Studies — wrote indicates that trust is developing.

Of course, trust is essential for any kind of healthy dialogue. The reason for the development of interreligious dialogue over the past few decades has been as a response to the level of *destructive criticism* so common to interchanges among adherents of the world's religions. To address this unacceptable level of conflict, it was necessary to step back and consciously adapt a stance of *silent humility* about and toward the religious other. As the dialogue movement developed, conversations began to punctuate the silence, conversations that hopefully demonstrated openness and understanding of our mutual pasts and intertwined futures. Years of this kind of openness leading to understanding make it possible to enter into a new era of dialogue, the era of *constructive criticism* made up of equal parts of honest commentary and unequivocal support.

We have moved through this idealized paradigm of responses very imperfectly of course. The level of destructive conflict is still unacceptably high, silent humility is sometimes in short supply, openness drowned out by self-interest, and constructive criticism imperfectly practiced. Yet we must move forward, experiencing flashes of epiphany and enlightenment as humility, openness, and mutuality ride the wings of developing trust.

The second observation — more a realization, actually — is that this form of interreligious interchange requires a high level of sophistication about religions other than one's own. It is hard to pin down the exact nature of this sophistication. It is not just knowledge about the other's religion that is required, although it is partly that. One cannot comment effectively about Buddhist meditation unless one has a certain fundamental understanding of what Buddhist meditation is. Christian prayer is not easy to define, but certain features of the practice are universally recognized among both theologians and practitioners. To do the kind of mutual evaluation required in this type of dialogue, basic levels of understanding are necessary.

The dialogue as we envision it, however, goes beyond knowledge. In our letter of invitation to participants, we made it clear we were also interested in writers who had some *experience* with the other religion's spiritual practice. As we received and evaluated submissions, it became clear that what gave the essays power and authority was the mixture of knowledge and experience of the others' spiritual practice. As you will see, it wasn't always the case that our writers had adopted meditative or prayer practice wholesale. But invariably their experience gained through learning about the practice led to changes: deeper, richer practice in their own tradition.

This kind of interaction has not been common among the world's religions in the past. We would be remiss not to acknowledge that a new day and age — a complicated new cultural context often captured in the word *globalization* — have created the conditions that make this sophisticated interchange possible. Religion is slowly but surely being decoupled from both nationality and ethnicity. This is happening more quickly in some places than in others. Regardless, it is creating a heady sense of freedom as far as religious identification is concerned. In such a setting, seeing other religions as resources for one's own is not only possible but desirable. Freedom to choose, however, requires discernment, the sophistication born of knowledge and experience and truth.

And so, this third observation is simply a recognition of the enormous creativity being shown as participants in this interreligious interchange craft ideas and practices faithful to their own traditions and to the integrity of borrowed knowledge and adaptive experiences.

We think the creativity will continue and build in the future. We are not moving toward one world religion but toward a community of religions that allows for full commitment in a context of openness, disagreement in a climate of respect.

BUDDHIST SPIRITUAL PRACTICE
AS SEEN BY CHRISTIANS

How I, a Christian, Have Learned from Buddhist Practice, or "The Frog Sat on the Lily Pad...Not Waiting"

FRANCES S. ADENEY
Louisville Presbyterian Theological Seminary

As a CHRISTIAN, I have practiced various forms of silent meditation. I remember sitting under the grand piano as a child of three, watching the sun flit through white curtains during our one-hour home communion service of the Plymouth Brethren. Most of the hour was spent in communal silence, gathered around a small table upon which was placed wine and bread. My memories of these meetings are filled with a sense of awe and presence.

I practiced a different kind of silent meditation as a young adult when I spent six weeks living on a beach in Greece. I saw few people apart from my two companions and the shepherdess who brought her flock to the meadow each day. I spent hours watching the waves or studying the grains of sand at my feet. I never missed a sunset.

At certain times of my life, there were more intentional, prayer-filled kinds of silent meditation. Wordless yearnings and grievings were brought to those meditations as I sought understanding and peace during times of illness, loss, and confusion. I wouldn't call any of those experiences Buddhist meditation. They were intentionally focused on either worshiping Christ or experiencing nature. There was no attempt to leave behind desires, no longing for emptiness, no intentional focus on being in the present moment, qualities that I associate with Buddhist meditation.

The first time I joined a group of people practicing Buddhist sitting was in 1997. Yet I felt like I had been doing this kind of silent meditating for years. Here is how that convergence came about.

During the early 1990s, while living in Indonesia, I frequently visited a Trappist monastery in central Java. The nuns there didn't practice Buddhism, but my spiritual director, a German priest who lived down the mountain, said to me, "Come and see." Father Hamma introduced me to sitting in a gentle non-technique-oriented way. He called it "contemplative prayer." I took up this practice daily during a difficult time of loss in my life. Spiritual retreats at the monastery up the mountain helped me learn to let go of what I could not hold onto in life. It was there that I began to experience the delight and calm that comes from a practice of meditative silence.

This silent meditation differed from other practices of silence that I had known in significant ways: (1) It was not focused on an interchange between God and myself. I was not listening for God's voice. I was not bringing my concerns to God. I was simply entering a place of silence. (2) It was not predicated on specific ideas about God or thoughts from writings in the Bible. I did not need to frame this time of silence with religious meanings. (3) It was not focused on an outcome. I neither expected nor did I ask for any changes in myself or the world.

Yet there were ways in which this practice of meditative silence was framed by my Christian faith. In taking up this practice, I felt I was intentionally entering God's presence. While not looking for spiritual experiences, I was somehow seeking life, and I did believe that God met me in those silent moments. More than once I had experiences that were "sightings" if not meetings with the Divine. During the seven years that I have practiced entering silence, the space that I enter has grown larger, and the conviction that I am entering and becoming part of God's presence deepens.

> The frog
> sat
> on the lily pad
> not waiting.

This Haiku poem resulted from one such experience. I had taken the bus out from the city. It dropped me at the foot of one of hundreds of small mountains in Java covered by lush greenery. The two-and-one-half-hour trek from the main road to the monastery took me through rice fields and small villages, over streams that ran under the road, and past hens and dogs who thought the road was theirs to sleep on and explore. I stopped, as usual, across from the elementary school to buy a bottle of water and some peanuts. Children gathered around me, and a few, curious enough to put aside their shyness, asked me my name, touched my skin.

That day I arrived at the gate of Gedono during mid-morning prayers. The sound of soprano voices wafted out of the chapel above me. Rather than entering, I seated myself by a small pool at the foot of the chapel steps. The sun brightened the lily pads in the dark pool, and I noticed a green frog sitting on one of them. Just sitting.

I decided to sit like that, allowing the sun to warm my back, staying quite still, completing my journey to this place of silent retreat. I felt that I need not go further. I had come there to be in silence. I need not enter the chapel and join in the singing of the Psalms. I need not wait for the sisters to come out of the chapel. I could begin. There was nothing to wait for. I sat still with the unmoving frog. The sounds of singing became distant. The mountain faded away. The whole world became the pond and me; I and the pond became the whole world.

During the past seven years, I have continued to practice the "contemplative prayer" that I learned from Father Hamma. I call it "entering silence." I've learned that it is indeed a form of Buddhist sitting. The attention to breath, the use of a holy word, the letting go of thoughts, the focus on the present, the importance of posture — these "techniques" prepare one for entering silence.

I use this practice alongside other forms of Christian prayer and meditation, seeing it as complementary rather than contradictory to practices of verbal prayer, meditative Bible reading, and community liturgies. As I evaluate this Buddhist practice as a Christian, I understand it as:

1. *A preparation for an encounter with the Divine.* Thomas Merton is said to have remarked that Western Christians could learn a lot about prayer from the East. This has been my experience with entering silence. I have occasionally, I believe, been taken beyond myself to a nonverbalizable encounter with what

is greater and deeper, and inclusive of my own being. In more ordinary experience, entering silence deepens my faith and calls from me a compassion for others and an appreciation of their worth and ways. I believe this too is a way of encountering the Divine.

As a Christian, I intentionally enter God's presence each time I practice silent meditation. Because I believe that God's Spirit meets me in a concrete spiritual way in meditation, my meditative experience is full of presence. It is not that what happens differs from the Buddhist experience; the intensity of deepened consciousness, the passing of time without awareness of its passing, the stillness of little breath, and the sense of etherealness of oneself and one's surroundings are similar. But the interpretation of what happens — that God configures God's self with me in the matrix of real spatiotemporal relationship — that is different (see Peter C. Hodgson, *God in History: Shapes of Freedom,* Nashville: Abingdon, 1989, 93).

I would not presume to say whether or not God meets the Buddhist in the same way. Revelation occurs in internal history, for Christians, our history as a Christian church (H. Richard Niebuhr, *The Meaning of Revelation,* New York: Macmillan, 1941, reprint ed. 1960, 44). The ontological realities of which we speak are confessionally understood from within our history and faith community, not from outside. Furthermore, respect for the Buddhist community requires that I not presume the activity of a personal God who is absent from most Buddhist theologies. But my evaluation of this practice, which I use as a Christian, leads me to conclude that encounter with God is a valued part of the process.

2. *A way of fostering self-understanding.* The experience of entering silence has allowed me to explore the deeper reaches of myself, gaining insights into areas of suppressed pain and anger and aiding me in finding direction in my life. I don't know why or how this happens, but it seems to be an experience that Buddhists and Jungians, as well as Jews and Christians, agree can spring from developing a habit of practicing silence.

My way of interpreting this process as a Christian focuses on the healing power of God's love and the efficacy of prayer. Jesus, according to the gospel of John, promised to send a Comforter, the Holy Spirit, to the community after his death. "Peace I leave with you; my peace I give to you," he said (John 14:27). I experience that peace in entering silence. In describing prayer, the apostle Paul said that when Christians don't know how to pray, "the Spirit intercedes for us with sighs too deep for words" (Rom. 8:27). Meditation, for me as a Christian, sometimes feels like sinking into a deep place of peace where all suffering is wordlessly heard and compassionately soothed.

Such experiences give me rest and provide energy for life's tasks. They also enable me to extend compassion to others who are hurt or oppressed. The Christian metaphor of drinking from deep wells of living water most closely describes this experience. Jesus said to the woman at the well, "Everyone who drinks of this water will thirst again, but whoever drinks of the water that I shall give will never thirst: the water that I shall give will become a spring of water in them, welling up to eternal life" (John 4:13–14). Entering silence is like drinking from a deep well of cool water. I don't think about it. I don't analyze what exactly happens or why this mystical water quenches my thirst. I come and drink.

3. *A form of discipline that puts into perspective individual transience and small-ness in relation to the universe and the Divine.* Entering silence helps me to get beneath the sometimes troubled waters of my daily life and lose myself in the vastness of the universe that cradles my life, although it does not always respond to my wishes.

The times spent at Gedono were times of letting go. Facing my father's death, accepting that continents separated me from my nearly grown children, and entering midlife were situations that required relinquishing control. Eventually, I knew, I would face my own death. My Christian faith helped me to open my hands, giving each love and life to God, accepting the inevitable losses while trusting God's wisdom. Silent meditation helped me in this process of letting go of attachments and deepening my connection with the depths of life that undergird me.

I learned the practice of Buddhist sitting at a Trappist monastery from a German Jesuit priest teaching Christian spiritual direction to Indonesian Catholics in Java. Perhaps that says something about the adaptability of the wisdom of the practice of Buddhist sitting. But the silence toward which this practice directs us does not belong to Buddhism or any tradition that adopts it. Rather, we belong to the silence and continue to search in innumerable ways for its embrace.

What I Know and Don't Know: A Christian Reflects on Buddhist Practice

MARY FROHLICH

Catholic Theological Union

T O REFLECT AND WRITE on spiritual practice for publication in an academic journal requires a delicate balancing act. It is not appropriate simply to recount one's experience; nor is it appropriate merely to theorize. I am assisted in this balancing act by a set of categories proposed some years ago by Walter Principe and generally accepted as standard now within the academic field of spirituality. Principe observed that spirituality operates on three interrelated yet distinct levels and that it is crucial for the academician to be clear about which level or levels are being presented. The three are: (1) experience; (2) articulation within wisdom traditions; (3) academic interpretation.[1] My understanding of what is desired in the present context is some of all three but with a primary emphasis on the second. What does Buddhist practice look like from my stance within my Christian "wisdom traditions"? Thus, this is the horizon within which I will present both experience and academic insights.

First a bit of autobiographical context. I became a Christian as a young adult, after having been raised in a secular humanist household. My first attempts at a form of meditation as a teenager came from reading Taoist books; in college I experimented with drugs (at that time this was often seen as "spiritual practice") and spent a couple of years very seriously practicing transcendental meditation. Only after all this did I seek baptism and church membership. Since then, my certainty that my call is to be a Christian has not wavered. I spent several years in a Carmelite contemplative monastery, and I now belong to another Roman Catholic religious order. Yet I have repeatedly been drawn to periods of engagement with various practices having Hindu and Buddhist roots.

This context is important to describe because I am aware that for me (and for many spiritual seekers today) there can never be a "pure" insertion in a single tradition. I reflected on that recently in an airplane at twenty-five thousand feet, looking down and seeing how totally human constructive activity has reshaped the contours of the land, the rivers, and everything that depends on them. I realized then that the same must be said of the inner contours of my soul. Nearing fifty, I bear the marks of everything that I have ever done or touched or suffered or known. As I approach this task of reflecting on Buddhist practice from the point of view of a Christian, I cannot do it as a pure outsider. My spiritual practice is Christian in its core, but it has been inextricably shaped by so many other influences — including varieties of Buddhist practice.

It is also important to acknowledge the limits of my knowledge about Buddhism and Buddhist practices. My academic exposure to Buddhism is about equivalent to an introductory undergraduate course. As for Buddhist practice, I have participated in a total of five weekend retreats, three one-week retreats, and one three-week retreat. These were all from either Vipassana (Insight Meditation) or Zen (Kwan Um or Diamond Sangha) traditions. Occasionally, I have also had even briefer exposure to other Buddhist traditions. I am very aware that there is much I do not know, or that perhaps I just plain misunderstand, about Buddhism. Yet dialogue requires that I honestly state my views, in their present form, with the hope that in the dialogical process what is misinformed or insensitive can eventually be corrected.

Spiritual practice (for Buddhists as well as Christians) involves many different kinds of practices. Practices of charity, such as hospitality or almsgiving, perhaps present the fewest obstacles to mutual understanding, because the practices may be generally similar in both traditions. The ritual practices of a religious tradition, on the other hand, can feel extremely alien to those who do not belong to that religious culture. Paul Hanvey has noted that our reaction to being confronted by an alien culture often proceeds through four stages: first, fascination with its exotic bizarreness; second, annoyance at its frustrating irrationality; third, intellectual knowledge; fourth, learning how to be at home.[2] My reflections on what I have experienced of Buddhist ritual practices would undoubtedly be complex, betraying elements of all four of these responses. The approach I will take, instead, is to focus primarily on interior practices such as meditation and prayer. My engagement with these has been long and deep; perhaps I am a bit closer to the "at home" stage here than with other kinds of practice.

I begin with a brief account of my personal daily practice of prayer and meditation. I usually spend fifteen to twenty minutes in the morning and twenty to forty minutes in the evening in my prayer corner. I sit in half lotus on a blanket and *zafu*, facing a small bench with a candle, a crucifix, and sometimes other objects. A Bible is beside me; sometimes there are other reading materials as well. In the morning, I usually read the scriptures for the day in *lectio divina* style — that is, going through the texts slowly a couple of times to see whether God seems to be "speaking" to me in some particular aspect of the daily word. If so, I reflect on that and what it may mean for the day. Then I spend the remaining time — at least five to ten minutes — in "sitting."

In the evening, most often the entire time is "sitting." I sit straight but comfortably on the *zafu*, place my intention toward Christ, and begin opening up. An eventful journey always takes place. Sometimes what happens involves a good deal of mental chatting (with Christ as my conversation partner) or side trips into interesting reflections. Other times I am drawn deep into memories, emotions, and physical tensions that need to be worked through. Still other times there are intense energies, blissful and seductive — or strange and frightening. My lodestar through all this is the intention of fidelity to Christ. This intention requires repeatedly letting go of whatever is attracting or holding me, insofar as it is not Christ. Yet this letting go is gentle and nonjudgmental about whatever is happening, because all of it is part of the trusting relationship. Chatting, reflecting, working through memories, or being possessed by energies — perhaps this is what is needed today. Receive it as gift — and let it go. The main thing is not to shift my core intention away from Christ. If I begin to pursue any value other than Christ — whether it is knowledge, pleasure, healing or anything else — I am in trouble.

In this practice, it seems as if the most profound and authentic moments (insofar as I can judge that) are those of "unknowing." Completely abandoned to Christ, I no longer know anything—and yet "know" that I am safe in him. In this state of abandoned trust, I am content with awareness that Christ is at work in and through me and that I do not have to do anything about it except let it be. An image that sometimes seems to express this is that of becoming a door for Christ: the door is empty, it is nothing, it does nothing, yet through the door passes the very Life of the universe.

How is this different from Buddhist practice? The obvious and central difference is that the core is faith in, and intention toward, Christ. Buddhist practices that I am familiar with usually enjoin some kind of "oneing" of intention by focus on the breath, a mantra, a mandala, a koan, or simply on the flow of consciousness. On one level this works in the same way as the single intention toward Christ, because both entail continually letting go of whatever else captures the attention. Yet the entire atmosphere is different, since the field in which one does the practice is simply one's own consciousness rather than a personal relationship of love and trust. Perhaps some element of the latter is provided to serious Buddhist practitioners who develop a deep and committed relationship with a particular teacher. Yet my impression is that Buddhist teachers ultimately do not encourage that kind of total trust. They are, after all, only human like the disciple; sooner or later the disciple has to accept that.

In my experience, Buddhist meditation practices are considerably more rigorous than most Christian interior practices (including mine). By this I mean that they place a greater emphasis on being vigilant about sticking clearly to the practice. If one is attending to the breath, anything else is to be let go—no excuses. Since as a Christian I experience myself in a personal relationship, I can be more gentle about the various ways in which that relationship may be playing out. Since Christ is incarnate as well as transcendent, thoughts, feelings, memories, and so on may be where he is, for now. Perhaps the danger of this more easygoing approach is that one can get caught up in a particular way of relating to Christ and not open up to the next step of letting it go for the sake of the yet deeper "unknowing." I have found that participating in the rigor of Buddhist practice has helped me to discover the importance of that dynamic of always, again, letting go.

Another way that Buddhist practices tend to be more rigorous is in the emphasis on long periods of immersion in interior practice. A Buddhist retreat normally seems to involve eight to twelve (or more) hours a day of meditation, with the rest of the time also spent in very interiorly focused ways. It is assumed that everyone who goes on such a retreat, regardless of their previous practice or level of spiritual openness, can do this and will benefit from it. On Christian retreats, however, even three or four hours of intensive interior prayer a day is regarded by most retreat directors as unusual and probably excessive. Of course, the Christian retreat also will include other forms of practice such as liturgy, spiritual talks, reflection on scripture, conversational prayer, and contemplation of nature. Yet after having participated in several very intensive Buddhist retreats, the Christian ones can seem just plain wimpy. One develops a taste for the intensity and depth of experience that is possible in those long hours — even though often much of it is intense restlessness and pain!

I find that I have to give a somewhat paradoxical evaluation to this passion for immersion in the inner world that is often found in those of us (both Buddhists and Christians) who have participated in intensive Buddhist practice. On the one hand, there are dimensions of contemplative development that probably cannot happen unless one devotes many long and rigorous hours to this kind of solitary swimming in the heavy seas of the interior life. Christians who are serious about opening up to the fullness of contemplative life almost have to take some of their swimming lessons from the East, where this is more commonly practiced. On the other hand, it seems to me that one of the things that very often happens (again, to both Buddhists and Christians) is an attachment to certain kinds of inner experiences. Buddhist meditation practices have the capacity to open up dimensions of the interior world that are incredibly fascinating and seductive, as well as some that are quite literally abysmal. I am not entirely sure how Buddhists evaluate the role these play in their spiritual journey, but for Christians they require great caution and discernment.

In relation to this, a comment in a recent *Buddhist-Christian Studies* book review caught my eye: "A Western woman alone in her apartment is far more radically alone than a Tibetan hermit meditating in a cave for thirty years. In the mind of the hermit the cave is populated with innumerable spirits. . . . "[3] Are "spirits" manifested in those powerful interior states that fascinate and seduce and even temporarily take over one's soul? Evagrius, a fourth-century Christian monk who is often noted as having some commonalities with Buddhism, seems to have thought so.[4] Perhaps the Buddhist presumes that the way is through them and that they are, in that sense, companions. In the New Testament and in the desert traditions of the early Christian centuries, however, there is a strong emphasis on how Christ casts out and conquers all *daimonia* (spirits). The Christian, then, must presume that the Holy Spirit of Christ supercedes all spirits; Christ alone is our companion and savior. This perhaps makes the inner context of Christian prayer paradoxically both more solitary *and* more radically communal — since, in Christ, we share divine life with the communion of saints throughout the ages.

Buddhist and Christian meditation practices, then, seem to ask for different kinds of rigor. Buddhist practice is more athletically demanding of time, capacity for physical and mental endurance, and concentrated focus. Christian practice, however, may be more demanding of "single-heartedness." It is a call to a gentle but uncompromising asceticism of the heart. Anything (even the spirits) may be the expression or messenger of our brother Christ, but nothing may shift our attention from loving him.

Having said all this, my final reflection has to return to "unknowing." I said earlier that this is the character of my most authentic and profound moments of interior practice. There is a long Christian tradition of the "cloud of unknowing," deriving from Gregory of Nyssa, Pseudo-Dionysius, and others, as well as from the fourteenth-century book of that title.[5] The more one knows God, the less one knows what one knows. The more one abandons oneself to God, the more one is "in the dark" about what God is up to; one lives only in trust and faith. In my participation in retreats with the Kwan Um school of Zen, I was struck with the repeated emphasis on "don't know mind." For these Zen practitioners, authentic practice is summed up in the simplicity and trust of a child. When they, deeply rooted in their own tradition, are granted a glimpse of this not-knowing, is it the same as when, embraced by Christ, I pass over into unknowing? I don't know.

Notes

1. Walter Principe, "Toward Defining Spirituality," *Studies in Religion/Sciences Religieuses* 12 (1983): 127–41; also idem, "Spirituality, Christian," in Michael Downey, ed., *The New Dictionary of Catholic Spirituality* (Collegeville, Minn.: Liturgical Press, 1993), 932–38.

2. Paul Hanvey, "Cross Cultural Awareness," in Elise Smith, ed., *Toward Internationalism* (Rowley, Mass.: Newbury House, 1979), 53.

3. *Buddhist-Christian Studies,* 19:231.

4. Evagrius Ponticus, *The Praktikos and Chapters on Prayer,* John Eudes Bamberger, trans. and ed. (Kalamazoo, Mich.: Cistercian Publications, 1981), esp. 3–10.

5. See James Walsh, "Introduction," in *The Cloud of Unknowing* (New York: Paulist, 1981).

On the Practice of Faith: A Lutheran's Interior Dialogue with Buddhism

Paul O. Ingram
Pacific Lutheran University

I EARN MY LIVING practicing the craft of history of religions. In Lutheran theological language, this is my "calling" and "vocation." I know this to be true because of how I was first opened to an amazing world of religious pluralism nearly forty years ago during my first undergraduate history of religions course. I am still amazed by this world and at times stunned to silence. The history of religions continues to inform my self-understanding and has recently become for me a primary mode of theological reflection and practice that intensely energizes both my exterior conceptual dialogue with Buddhist doctrine and teaching and my interior dialogue with Buddhist meditative practice.[1]

So my vocation is teaching an academic field of inquiry I love to young people as I engage in research and writing. I am paid for doing this by a university related to the Evangelical Lutheran Church in America that bills itself as a "new American university" located in one of the most culturally pluralistic and beautiful regions in the United States. While I'm not sure what a "new American university" is, I am certain I have a great gig. I am equally convinced that my professional life constitutes for me some of the evidence of the grace that Christian tradition in general — and Luther's theology in particular — describe as flowing "in, with, and under" this universe like a waterfall, like a tidal wave.

Admittedly, all this is highly confessional, perhaps too confessional, for a scholar's essay on how reflection on Buddhist traditions of practice has informed his practice. Yet when it comes down to it, all theological reflection — as well as the discipline of practice itself — is confessional. We can only write about our particular interior journey as it is informed by the particular community of faith that gives context to our practice, for it is not probable that most persons can be religious in general, but only in particular.[2] After all, Carmelite nuns do not ordinarily seek or experience nonduality with the Buddha Nature, nor do Buddhist nuns ordinarily seek or experience interior union with Christ the Bridegroom. Yet sometimes a few historians of religions and a few Christian theologians and Buddhist philosophers are able to participate in communities of faith and practice other than their own. This too seems to me a sign of grace.

I have learned two lessons from interior dialogue with Buddhists as this shakes out in my particular practice. First, our interior journeys lead us through time — forward and back, seldom in a straight line, most often in spirals. Each of us is moving and changing in relationship to others and to the world, and, if one is grasped by Christian faith, to God, or if grasped by Buddhist faith (*srada*), the Dharma.[3] As we discover what our interior journeys teach us, we remember; remembering, we discover; and most intensely do we discover when our separate journeys converge. It is at spots of Christian and Buddhist convergence that I have experienced the most dramatic and creatively transformative processes of interreligious dialogue.

Second, as a Lutheran it strikes me as a bit glib to suggest that the focus of practice is "God" or, if Buddhist, "Emptiness," because I often feel intellectually and emotionally blindsided by what people who practice mean by these words. The question, always an epistemological one, is what do these terms mean as we practice whatever we practice. Plenty of theological-philosophical propositions can be strung together to answer this question, and, I think, it is important to guide practice by theological-philosophical reflection. But we must never cling to belief in propositions, because the moment we do, they will hide the reality to which they point. Conceptualizing and believing in rational propositions is a necessary beginning because it is a form of "faith seeking understanding." But faith is never, in Christian or Buddhist tradition, identical with belief in propositions. Faith implies being grasped by and betting one's life on; that is, trusting the reality to which propositions may sometimes point — a grasp that goes beyond propositions, is not caused by propositions, yet cannot be experienced nonpropositionally, since even the statement "God" or "Emptiness is beyond the grasp of language" is still a "proposition."

Of course, much also depends on the meaning of "practice." The clearest discussion of the meaning of "practice" I have found within the context of Buddhist-Christian dialogue is a remarkable essay written by John C. Maraldo entitled "The Hermeneutics of Practice in Dogen and Francis of Assisi."[4] Maraldo notes that the popular understanding of practice is instrumental: practice (*praxis*) is something different from theory (*theoria*); theory and theoretical knowledge are ends in themselves; practice is an end outside itself.[5] Much discussion of practice within the context of Buddhist-Christian dialogue assumes this popular understanding. For example, one often hears from Zen Buddhists and advocates of Christian "spirituality" that doctrines are meaningless, that the mind should be emptied of such theoretical stuff so that what's *really* real about reality can be experienced directly by a mind unfettered by theoretical constructions. Seen from this perspective, practice is an instrumental means of achieving something we don't think we have. So one practices meditation or contemplative prayer as a method to achieve a "beyond-all-language" experience of awakening or union with God.

Such instrumental understandings that bifurcate practice from achievement of a goal presuppose that we need to do something to achieve whatever it is we don't think we have, as if we were on the outside of our lives looking in. But this does not quite square with Christian contemplative traditions and Buddhist meditative traditions, and it is certainly contrary to Luther's teaching about faith and grace and his rejection of all "works" as instrumental means of creating a redemptive relationship with God. Buddhist tradition, Roman Catholic and Orthodox contemplative tradition, and mainline Protestant tradition agree: we have everything we are ever going to have, and there is nothing to gain — absolutely nothing — through practice, because practice and attainment are nondual. For me as a Lutheran Christian, therefore, religious practice is the disciplined performance of faith without regard to achieving goals, if you will, a kind of Christian "actionless-action" (Chinese, *wu-wei*), since faith is not something I decide to "have" by any act of the will to believe. One *finds* oneself in a state of faith, one does not *"practice"* oneself into a state of faith, since there is no time when we or any other thing or event in the universe is ever separated from God — at least according to the Genesis creation story as read through the prologue of the Gospel of John.

Of course, this presupposes Luther's teaching that grace operates universally at all times and in all places in this universe. For me, this means that if one is engaged in a religious practice, one is drawn to it by grace through faith alone, which means there is nothing to gain by practice that one does not already have. Within Buddhist tradition, Shinran's teaching that even awakening itself is created in us by Amida Buddha's compassionate "other-power" points to a parallel Buddhist understanding of the experience of the utter interdependence of grace, faith, and practice.[6]

Any activity that takes practice to be performed skillfully will do to illustrate what I mean. Recall such activities as practicing a musical instrument or dance, learning a language, practicing a martial art, doing floral arrangement or the tea ceremony, or writing poetry. To practice these activities requires repeated effort and concentrated performance. Such activities are daily disciplines exercised for no other reason than their performance — unless one is a novice who mistakenly interprets practice as different from skilled performance. But as an activity becomes "practiced" and proficient performance is acquired, the gap between what we will and what we do disappears. "It may even be said that during any practice there is no room for desires or intentions which separate our present performance from an imagined ideal, what we are doing from how we wish we were doing it."[7] Consequently, my particular "practice" has evolved into three interdependent forms: (1) theological reflection; (2) centering prayer; and (3) social engagement.

According to my colleague, Patricia O'Connell Killen, theological reflection is a discipline that becomes an art by its practice. She defines "theological reflection" as: "the discipline of exploring individual and corporate experience in conversation with the wisdom of a religious heritage. The conversation is a genuine dialogue that seeks to hear from our own beliefs, actions, and perspectives, as well as those of the tradition. It respects the integrity of both. Theological reflection therefore may confirm, challenge, clarify, and expand how we understand our own experience and how we understand the religious tradition. The outcome is new truth and meaning for living."[8]

While the above quotation was written from a Roman Catholic perspective, what it says about theological reflection can be extended with appropriate modifications to other religious traditions, because the structure of the art of theological reflection is, for me, a dialogical process with five interdependent movements: (1) through reading a text, one enters his or her *experience* and (2) encounters *feelings* or *emotional responses* engendered by the text; (3) paying attention to these feelings generates *images;* (4) attending and questioning images may lead to *insight;* (5) insight leads, if we are willing, to *action,* part of the meaning of which for me is "social engagement."[9]

The art of theological reflection is not identical with academic theology, although my commitment to academic theological discourse continues to contextualize my particular practice of theological reflection. Nor is the art of theological reflection identical with what Catholic monastic theology calls *lectio divina* ("divine reading"), although there are similarities. Specifically, I tend to focus on Christian and non-Christian texts as well as remembered conversations and experiences that seem to me transformative. Part of my practice is to read the New Testament through once a year, usually in the summer when I have more quiet time, guided by a single question.[10] My reasons are both scholarly and personal: I think historians of religions must first understand and appreciate their own religious tradition before they are in a position to adequately understand and appreciate religious traditions other than their own. Furthermore, practice needs to be grounded in the foundational traditions of one's community.

I also include the Psalms and other texts from the Hebrew Bible as objects of — theological reflection, as well as Buddhist texts like Santideva's *Bodhicaryavatara* ("Entering the Path of Enlightenment"), the writings of Martin Luther and Martin Luther King; the poetry of William Butler Yeats and T. S. Eliot; the writings of Thich Nhat Hahn and Annie Dillard; the journals of Thomas Merton, and most recently, the mystical theology of thirteenth-century women mystics like Marguerite Porete. The writings of John Cobb, Wilfred Cantwell Smith, Huston Smith, and John Hick; the novels of John Steinbeck and my friend Jack Cady; the Buddhist reflections of Sallie King and Rita Gross; and the theology of religions of Paul Knitter — so deeply energized by his passion for social engagement — are also examples of texts I have appropriated for theological reflection.

For me the process involves keeping a journal, since I am convinced that writing itself is a mode of meditation and that we never adequately understand a thing until we write it down. I do not engage in this practice expecting specific experiences or insights. Instead, I try to allow the process to take me where it takes me, like going on a journey without a destination or map. So as I read a text during this practice, I begin by reflecting on the experience the text occasions and try to accurately describe its inner and outer dimensions—what the particular experience is to me and its objective content—in order to be fully aware of the source and nature of the experience. In other words, the intent is to attend to the experience's positive, negative, or neutral "emotional tone"—in Japanese, its *mono no aware*—by nonjudgmentally describing it, simply noting what the feelings are, in order to live consciously "inside" the experience because this is the best position from which to reflect.

By entering an experience and narrating it nonjudgmentally, one discovers that it is drenched with feeling. This is so — probably in disagreement with standard Buddhist teaching — because our capacity to feel, to respond with our entire being to reality, is the essence of our nature as enfleshed persons. As such, feelings are embodied affective and intelligent responses to reality as we encounter it, so that feelings join mind and body and are the most human responses to reality, meaning "the way things really are." That is, through feelings, we encounter reality incarnated in our lives.[11]

This aspect of theological reflection, then, involves paying close attention to feelings, because they embody a holistic response to our existence and are a source of creative insight. It is a process full of promise and often full of danger. The danger comes in two ways: (1) being overwhelmed and mired in feelings so that we subjectively grovel in them, or (2) being deadened to them. Both responses block insight. So the stage of attending to feelings involves being aware of them, without denying them or clinging to them, so that they can be identified clearly and accurately.

The next step entails giving shape and voice to feelings in the language of symbolic imagery. People do this in normal conversation all the time, as, for example, when my grandfather would say of a person he thought was ignorant, "He wouldn't know sheep shit from raisins if it was in the same pie," or when a sad person says,"I feel like a motherless child," or when someone describes her friend as having "a heart of gold." Images work differently than conceptual language. Images are more total, more closely tied to feelings, and less rationalized. Images create ways for feelings to be included in our world of meaning, thereby expanding our world by more immediate inclusion of new experience.

Sometimes musing on an image pushes us to new insights and frees us to respond to reality in ways never before imagined, because images can compress many aspects of a situation into an integrated, intense, wholeness and, at the same time, open us to new angles of vision. In the process, images help us break free from habitual ways of interpreting our lives by propelling us to discover new meanings. At other times, pondering an image leads to unexpected surprises. That is, images can capture the core of a situation — by shifting from the original descriptive narrative to a symbolic structure. In this way, they can engender insights and open doors to new ways of apprehension and self-awareness. Powerful insights can also engender action in the form of social engagement, consideration of which will be given after a brief description of centering prayer.[12]

Centering prayer is a method of refining one's intuitive faculties so that one can more easily enter contemplative prayer. Thomas Keating describes this as developing one's relationship with God to the point of communing beyond words, thoughts, feelings, and the multiplication of acts; "a process of moving from the simplified activity of waiting upon God to the ever-increasing predominance of the Gifts of the Spirit as the source of one's prayer."[13]

Centering prayer has much in common with certain aspects of Buddhist meditation, especially *zazen,* since unlike theological reflection, centering prayer is a discipline designed to withdraw attention away from the ordinary flow of conscious thoughts and feelings through which we tend to identify our selves. It aims to expand awareness of a deeper dimension of selfhood not completely sayable in words, yet to which words can symbolically point. Mahayana Buddhists call this dimension of selfhood the "true Self." According to Christian mystical theology, the true Self is the image of God in which every human being — in my opinion, all things — are created. So centering prayer, as I understand it, is a method of deepening the experience of interdependence, which in Christian teaching is affirmed theologically by the doctrines of creation and incarnation. Traditional Catholic theology understands centering prayer as preparatory to "contemplation," that process whereby the *image* of God incarnated in us as our true Self is transformed by grace into a *likeness* of God, so that we might apprehend the created universe as God apprehends it and love all things accordingly.

The technical details of my particular practice of centering prayer are fairly simple. For two thirty-minute periods a day — morning and evening — I take a comfortable sitting position in a quiet place, while avoiding positions that cut off circulation so that bodily discomfort will not block concentration. I begin by taking a few deep breaths and, while breathing slowly and evenly, shut my eyes and begin withdrawing my senses from ordinary activity. With closed eyes, I bring to conscious attention what Thomas Keating calls a "sacred word" that expresses my intention of opening and surrendering to God. I don't repeat this word aloud but rather use it as an interior object of concentration.

The purpose here is not to suppress conscious thoughts and feelings, because that is not possible. The intention is to "observe" thoughts and feelings as they pass in review without stopping them or holding on to them. Whenever I catch myself holding on to a thought or feeling, I gently bring the sacred word into conscious focus until the thought or idea moves on. In this way, as the stream of conscious thoughts and feelings is quieted, one gradually becomes centered and open to whatever there is beyond the limitations of thoughts and our emotional responses to them.

For me, then, centering prayer is essentially an exercise in letting go, a method of allowing, without forcing, my ordinary train of thoughts and feelings to flow out. It is a kind of waiting without expectation designed to bring the interdependence of the present fully and consciously into focal awareness. According to Thomas Keating, practicing centering prayer with expectations or goals takes us out of the present and projects us into an imagined future that is most probably a reflection of our present ego trips. So centering prayer is a method of waking up to the presence of God in, with, and under the present interdependent moment without attachment to or anxiety about the future. Thomas Merton described this practice as "Entering the Silence"[14] — a process that does not require being a monk or a nun and, from both a Christian and Buddhist perspective, always energizes social engagement.

One of the important lessons I have learned from students and colleagues practiced in social engagement is that interreligious dialogue is not merely an abstract conversation between religious persons on this or that doctrine. Interreligious dialogue — as well as the practice of theological reflection and centering prayer — requires and energizes involvement in the rough-and-tumble of historical, political, and economic existence. Or to paraphrase the

Epistle of James, "theological reflection, centering prayer, and interreligious dialogue without works is dead" for the same reasons that "faith without works is dead." For me, a central point of the practice of faith is the liberation of human beings and all creatures in nature from forces of oppression and injustice and the mutual creative transformation of persons in community with nature. Both the wisdom that Buddhists affirm is engendered by awakening and the Christian doctrines of creation and incarnation point to the utter interdependency of all things and events at every moment of space-time — a notion also affirmed by contemporary physics and biology in distinctively scientific terms.[15] Awareness of interdependency, in turn, engenders social engagement, because awareness of interdependence and social engagement are themselves interdependent. Thus we experience the suffering of others as our suffering, the oppression of others as our oppression, the oppression of nature as our oppression, and the liberation of others as our liberation — and thereby we become empowered for social engagement.

Consequently, any religious practice needs to include focus on practical issues that are not religion-specific or culture-specific, meaning issues that confront all human beings regardless of what religious or secular label persons wear. That is, my running thesis about practice is in agreement with Christians like Martin Luther, Martin Luther King, and Mother Theresa; the Vietnamese Buddhist monk Thich Nhat Hahn and the Thai Buddhist layman Sulak Siveraksa; the Hindu sage and activist Mahatma Gandhi; as well as Jewish and Islamic calls that we struggle for justice in obedience to Torah or surrender to Allah guided by the *Qur'an;* namely, that religious faith and practice do not separate us from the world. The practice of faith throws us *into* the world's rough-and-tumble-struggle for peace and justice; any practice that refuses to wrestle with the world's injustices is as impotent as it is self-serving. Accordingly, whatever practice we follow needs to be guided by a concern for the liberation of all sentient beings, for as both Christian and Buddhist teaching affirm, we are all in this together. Distinctively Christian practices and, I suspect, distinctively Buddhist practices cannot have it any other way, because in an interdependently processive universe, there is no other way.

NOTES

1. See my book *Wrestling with the Ox: A Theology of Religious Experience* (New York: Continuum, 1997).

2. This is a modified restatement of an observation by George Santanya. See *Interpretations of Poetry and Religion* (New York: Harper Tourchbooks, 1957), chapter 9.

3. See Robert Traer, "Faith in the Buddhist Tradition," *Buddhist-Christian Studies* 11 (1991): 85–120.

4. See Paul O. Ingram and Frederick J. Streng, eds., *Buddhist-Christian Dialogue: Essays in Mutual Renewal and Transformation* (Honolulu: University of Hawai'i Press, 1986), 53–74.

5. Ibid., 54–55.

6. I have made note of these parallels in several past publications. See my *The Dharma of Faith* (Washington, D.C.: University Press of America, 1977), chapter 4; "Shinran Shonin and Martin Luther: A Soteriological Comparison," *Journal of the American Academy of Religion* 39 (December 1971): 447–80.

7. Ingram and Streng, *Buddhist-Christian Dialogue*, 54.

8. Patricia O'Connell Killen, *The Art of Theological Reflection* (New York: Crossroad, 1994), viii.

9. Ibid., chapter 2.

10. Terry Muck introduced me to this practice over dinner in New Orleans in 1997. My question for this year was engendered by the death of my father in April: what does the Jesus saying, "To live your life you must first lose it" mean?

11. Killen, *The Art of Theological Reflection*, chapter 2.

12. Ibid.

13. Thomas Keating, *Open Mind, Open Heart* (New York: Continuum, 1997), 146.

14. Thomas Merton, *Entering the Silence: The Journals of Thomas Merton,* 2, ed. Jonathan Montaldo (San Francisco: HarperSanFrancisco, 1996).

15. See Arthur Peacocke, *Theology for a Scientific Age* (Minneapolis: Fortress Press, 1993), 39–43, for a wonderful summary of the current consensus among scientists regarding the interdependent and interconnected structure of the physical universe.

Readiness:
Preparing for the Path

TERRY C. MUCK

Asbury Theological Seminary

O NE IMPORTANT LESSON I learned from studying the way early Buddhist monks practiced the spiritual life was the lesson of readiness.[1] Before a person can make any progress on the spiritual path of his or her choice, they must be ready to undertake the path. I have come to see readiness as the foundational step on any religion's spiritual path.

Let me tell you how I came to this understanding in the specific case of Theravada Buddhism, and then I will explain how I have generalized that understanding to my own Christian tradition and beyond.

Buddhaghosa, the great early commentator on and synthesizer of the Pali Buddhist tradition, divided his classic work on the *dhamma,* the *Visuddhimagga,* into three stages: *sila,* or morality; *samadhi,* or concentration; and *panna,* or wisdom.[2] It is clear from his exposition that Buddhaghosa considered *sila* (morality) foundational to the spiritual path: "When a wise man, established well in morality, / Develops concentration and wisdom, / Then as a monk ardent and sagacious / He succeeds in disentangling this tangle."[3] Buddhaghosa advocated the moral life, as the foundation for the spiritual life. Until one establishes *sila,* or morality, progress in meditation was problematic.[4]

Of course, it is important to understand what Buddhaghosa meant by morality. In the *Visuddhimagga* he defined it this way: "Morality is intentionally chosen states present in one who abstains from killing, etc. or in one who fulfills the practice of the *Vinaya.* "[5] For Buddhaghosa, consciously choosing not to do certain things and then not doing them creates predictable states in a person that collectively create a condition he called morality. Those states of being are required in order to go on to attain the higher states of spiritual practice.

Sila took various forms and content. For the layperson it meant following as best one could five basic rules: no killing, no stealing, no lying, faithfulness in relationships, and abstaining from alcoholic beverages.[6] For the novice monk (and spiritually advanced laypersons), five additional rules were added: no untimely meals; no dancing, singing, music, or theater; no flowers, perfumes, and jewelry; no high seats; and no handling of gold and silver.[7] But *sila* for the monk was also defined by a longer list of 227 rules, called the *Patimokkha,* and narrative and commentary added to those rules, together called the *Vinaya-Pitaka.*[8]

The content of *sila* was not static — or perhaps it is better to say that it had a certain amount of flexibility. But it was implicitly acknowledged in the early texts that no matter what the exact form morality took, the life devoted to morality took effort. A person had to want to follow it. Thus, a decision had to be made to practice *sila* in preparation for *samadhi* and *panna.*

The nature of this decision, what I have come to call readiness, was what interested me most about the Buddhist spiritual path. The Pali texts divide readiness into two component parts: (1) *viriya,* or energy, and (2) *saddha,* or confidence (sometimes translated as faith, a confusing translation because the word "faith" is so closely associated with Christian doctrine and experience, where it means something quite different from *saddha*). In the Pali texts, then, these two elements are often paired in passages describing requirements for engaging *dhamma.* For example, both confidence and energy are listed as two of the five factors leading to success in spiritual wrestling.[9] In this passage in the *Digha Nikaya,* confidence (*saddha*) is defined as "believing in the Buddha's Enlightenment — thus is the Exalted One: he is Arahant fully awakened, wisdom he has, and righteousness; he is the Well-Farer; he has knowledge of the worlds; he is the supreme driver of men willing to be tamed; the teacher of devas and men; the Awakened and Exalted One."[10] Energy (*viriya*) is defined as "maintaining a flow of energy in eliminating wrong states of mind and evoking good states, vigorous, strongly reaching out, not shirking toil with respect to good states of mind."[11] These definitions indicate that a certain amount of both confidence and energy are required in order to undertake the path.

To be sure, the Buddha did not require or even ask for commitment based on the authority of his person. He also did not demand that prior allegiance to his teaching was a necessary starting point. This is an important point, because the Buddha taught that his teaching unlocked the secrets to overcoming suffering. He taught that this teaching was universal, the one, true way (*ekayamo maggo*): "The one and only path, monks, leading to the purification of beings... is that of the fourfold setting up of mindfulness (that is, the teaching of the Buddha)."[12] But he never tired of cautioning his listeners that one must follow the path not because he taught it but because they heard about it (or read about it) and tried it enough so that they came to have confidence in it enough to devote the requisite energies to its practice — that is, confidence in the path as they experienced it.[13]

This was readiness for the Buddha. A person comes and hears the teaching (*ehi passiko*), and that hearing creates the confidence that in turn creates the energy to develop morality, the foundation of spiritual life.[14] Developing such confidence as a result of a teaching means that the content of the teaching must be very important. The Buddha taught that we see the world in such a way as to create suffering. We see certain features of the world, features we experience as pleasurable, as permanent. When they turn out to be impermanent, we suffer at their loss. We see ourselves, our *atman,* as having an eternal essence. We suffer over that, because maintaining and nurturing the ego required for such an essence leads us to practice behaviors that are destructive of others: hatred, ill will, and greed, as the Pali texts summarize it.[15] The Buddha taught that we behave that way out of ignorance — we don't understand the basic lessons of impermanence and no-self. To practice the spiritual life we must come to an understanding of no-self (*anatta*). To practice the spiritual life, we must come to a basic understanding of our lack. Readiness means we understand we have that lack. People who are ready undertake the path. People who are not ready don't.

As I will argue in the next section, I think readiness may be common to many religious traditions and their spiritual practices. I, however, a Christian, learned this particular lesson from Buddhism, the focus of my scholarly study, not from Christianity. I wonder why? I can think of two possible reasons, one related to the Buddhism I studied, one to the Christianity I confess.

Studying a religion that is not one's own presents one with new and different ideas. Because these ideas are new and different they do not immediately fit into the carefully constructed belief structure of one's tradition. This creates dissonance, which in turn demands intellectual energy to resolve. The resolution can take many forms: rejection of the ideas as false, a widening of one's belief structure to accommodate them, a change in one's belief structure as a different truth becomes evident. Regardless of the outcome, however, new ideas force action to resolve the tension created by "wild facts," as William James called them.[16]

One of the wild facts of Buddhism's spiritual practice that I studied was the idea that morality was the foundation upon which spiritual progress was built. At first thought it seemed to me that Christianity taught something quite different — that morality was the *result* of spiritual practice, not its foundation. At first I thought of New Testament passages that listed the fruits of the spirit — love, joy, peace, patience, kindness, goodness, faithfulness, gentleness, and self-control.[17] Fruit means the end of a season of growth, not its beginning or root. How could morality be considered a foundation?

I had also always considered morality to be a sign that all was well with one's spiritual life. A healthy tree produces good fruit, a dying tree none. Morality was a sign that one's relationships with God, world, and neighbor were on target, while moral dissolution signaled the opposite.[18] This also seemed at odds with Buddhaghosa's comments on the moral foundation.

This dissonance set me on a course of study that included much more reading on Buddhism, a reexamination of my Christian beliefs, a broader and richer understanding of the idea of morality and its function in the spiritual life, and the concept of readiness that I sketched out in the first section of this paper and will complete in the last.

A second possible reason that I learned the lesson of readiness from Buddhism and not Christianity had to do with the intensity of my Christian beliefs. I think Christianity is the one, true way (just as the Buddha taught that *dhamma* was the *ekayamo maggo,* the one true path) and that following it makes it possible for us to successfully address life's problems. Because these beliefs are central to the way I live my life, they have become habitual. That is, they order my life in such a way that is largely unconscious. I do not reflect upon them unless "crisis" forces it.

Studying Buddhism and its teaching on morality and morality's relationship to the spiritual life created such a crisis for me. The idea that morality was the foundation and not the fruit of spiritual practice did not fit. After a long course of study too detailed to relate here, I came to see morality as having a dual role — as fruit *and* root of the spiritual life. As root it represents readiness, the conscious and willful effort to change, to prepare oneself for new patterns, to fill the lack in one's life. It does indeed take both confidence and energy to prepare the soil of one's life for new growth. As fruit, morality represents the habitual and largely unconscious way of living that results from following the path.

I was motivated to learn the lesson of readiness by the crisis presented to me by a study of Buddhism.

As Paul Ingram points out in his book *Wrestling with the Ox,* the third picture in the series of twelve Ox-Herding pictures used by Zen meditators to depict the spiritual path represents readiness: "The third Ox-Herding picture, 'Seeing the Ox,' depicts the man in process of discovering the whereabouts of his ox by the sounds he hears and the shadows he glimpses in the bushes. For the first time . . . he is beginning to 'see into the nature of things.' "[19] In John Bunyan's *Pilgrim's Progress,* the decision to undertake the path is characterized by a man reading the "book of life" and discovering that "both you and myself will come to ruin unless some way can be found for us to escape. I haven't found the way yet."[20] But he has found the resolve to get on the path. He has achieved readiness. Once my study of Buddhism suggested the concept of readiness to me, I began to see it everywhere. It emerged in many of the religious traditions I study. Over a period of time, I developed a sort of phenomenology of spiritual readiness. The concept appeared to have validity across religious tradition lines, although I realize that my way of expressing it is still captive to my Christian and Western context. Still, in abbreviated form, the dynamics of readiness has the following five stages:

1. All religions teach that the human condition has an element of lack or suffering;

2. Suffering can be traced to cosmological (theological) factors, but the form it takes is influenced by psychological states and cultural conditions;

3. The religions teach that suffering persists, in part at least, because most human beings resist, for whatever reason, the road to liberation from suffering;

4. The road away from suffering is paved with the understanding of religious (theological), psychological, and sociocultural factors that force it to persist;

5. A required step (not always the first step, but a very early one) is for the individual religious and the religious community to want to change. Spiritual practice, therefore, requires as an initiatory step a readiness to approach the transcendent.

Readiness, as revealed in specific religious practices, takes many forms. For some religious traditions, it takes the form of restraint. One thinks, for example, of the *yamas* listed in Patanjali's *Yoga Aphorisms*: nonviolence, nonlying, continence, simplicity of lifestyle.[21] Or the Jewish and Christian Ten Commandments.[22] Or some of the 227 rules of the Buddhist *Patimokkha* recited fortnightly by faithful *bhikkhus*.[23] These "don'ts" of religious spiritual life create readiness in their practitioners to absorb and realize the higher wisdoms of the path.

For some religious traditions, readiness spiritual practices take the form of positive deeds of action. One thinks, for example of the *niyamas* listed in Patanjali's *Yoga Aphorisms* (listed immediately after the *yamas*): purification, contentment, devotion to God.[24] Or the prescriptions of many of the passages of the Jewish Torah.[25] Or the purification of the Muslim *wudu* — the washing and meditation that prepares one for prayers and worship.[26]

For some religious traditions, readiness practice takes the form of individual examinations of conscious and unconscious behavior/belief. One thinks of Ignatius Loyola's examen, the four-step questioning one does at the end of the day regarding one's behavior.[27] To be sure, something like the *yamas* and *niyamas* could be used in similar examination of one's conscience. Prayer can take a similar form for Christians.

Examinations can also be corporate. The aforementioned fortnightly recitation of the *Patimokkha* by Theravada Buddhist *bhikkhus* is done in community. The Roman Catholic confessional is done to a priest. Presbyterians begin every worship service with a prayer of confession, to clear the decks of moral detritus so that worship can proceed apace. Clearly there is no shortage of practices designed to prompt and provoke readiness for spiritual practice, and the variety extends to almost all the borders of religious traditions.

This pervasiveness suggests application. First, it suggests an intriguing topic of conversation for interreligious interchanges. It seems to refer to a common human experience of a watershed moment. Who would not like to talk about that moment in time when they rearranged their priorities, did a lifestyle about-face, and stepped on the path. Who would not like to listen to someone else talk about their moment? Such discussions are compelling religious drama.

Second, the explanations of and rationales for readiness are diverse. The religious people of the world do not hold these in common. Who would not like to talk about their reasons and rationales and listen to those who have other understandings? Out of such conversations, new constructions emerge. And life becomes richer.

Notes

1. See my "From Discipline to Understanding: The Pali Vinaya Pitaka as Paradigm for Religious Studies Methodology," in *The Comity and Grace of Method: Festschrift for Edmund Perry*, ed. Thomas Ryba, George Bond, and Herman Tull (Evanston, Ill.: Northwestern University Press, 2000).

2. Buddhaghosa's *Visuddhimagga* has been translated by two scholars: Pe Maung Tin, trans., *The Path of Purity* (London: Luzac and Company, 1971), and Bhikkhu Nanamoli, trans., *The Path of Purification* (Kandy, Sri Lanka: Buddhist Publication Society, 1975).

3. *Visuddhimagga*, 1. Translation mine.

4. "He who is possessed of constant morality, has wisdom, and is concentrated, is strenuous and diligent as well, will cross the flood so difficult to cross." *Kindred Sayings*, vol. 1 (London: Luzac and Company, 1971), 76.

5. *Visuddhimagga*, 6. Translation mine.

6. H. Saddhatissa, *Buddhist Ethics: Essence of Buddhism* (New York: George Braziller, 1970), 87.

7. Saddhatissa, 110–12.

8. *The Book of the Discipline*, 6 vols., trans. I. B. Horner (London: Luzac and Company, 1963–71).

9. *Dialogues of the Buddha (Digha Nikaya)*, trans. T. W. and C. A. F. Rhys Davids (London: Luzac and Company, 1971), 226–27.

10. Ibid., 227.

11. Ibid.

12. "Mahasatipatthanasutta," in *Dialogues of the Buddha II (Digha Nikaya)*, trans. T. W. Rhys Davids (London: Luzac and Company, 1971), 327.

13. In a way the Buddha's confidence in himself modeled the confidence he expected of his followers. He saw himself as a good teacher: "For me there is no teacher, one like me does not exist. In the world with its devas, no one equals me. For I am perfected in the world, a teacher supreme am I, I alone am all-awakened." "Ariapariyesanasutta," in *Middle Length Sayings I (Majjhima Nikaya),* trans. I. B. Horner (London: Luzac and Company, 1967), 215. Yet the Buddha cautioned his followers not to consider confidence salvific in any way. To recognize him as a good teacher was simply a starting point.

14. *Ehi passako,* "come and see," is used in a stock phrase to describe the teaching of the Buddha and our response to it: "Well proclaimed by the Exalted One is the dhamma, seen in this life, a thing not involving time, inviting one to come and see, leading onward, to be known for themselves by the wise." "Janavasabhasuttanta," in *Dialogues of the Buddha II (Digha Nikaya)* (London: Luzac and Company, 1971), 250, and elsewhere in the Pali texts.

15. Han F. de Wit, *The Spiritual Path,* trans. Henry Jansen and Lucia Hofland-Jansen (Pittsburgh: Duquesne University Press, 1999).

16. James understood the psychology of religious change to involve a dynamic between unconscious, innate needs and conscious, ideal goals. The interplay between these two at first creates a divided self, but then produces absolute needs and irresistible goals that are compatible and become the unified self. William James, *Varieties of Religious Experience* (New York: Simon and Schuster, 1997), 170ff.

17. This list is from Galatians 5:22, *NIV Study Bible* (Grand Rapids, Mich.: Zondervan Publishing House, 1985), 1787.

18. The story is told of Jesus that upon passing a fig tree that was not producing any fruit, he cursed the tree — "May you never bear fruit again!" — and the tree withered. Matthew 21:18–19, *NIV Study Bible* (Grand Rapids, Mich.: Zondervan Publishing House, 1985), 1472.

19. Paul Ingram, *Wrestling with the Ox: A Theology of Religious Experience* (New York: Continuum, 1999), 55.

20. John Bunyan, *Pilgrim's Progress,* ed. Hal M. Helms (Orleans, Mass.: Paraclete Press, 1982), 115–16.

21. *A Sourcebook in Indian Philosophy,* ed. Sarvepalli Radhakrishnan and Charles Moore (Princeton, N.J.: Princeton University Press, 1957), 453–54.

22. See Exodus 20:1–17, *NIV Study Bible* (Grand Rapids, Mich.: Zondervan Publishing House, 1985), 115–16.

23. Charles S. Prebish, *Buddhist Monastic Discipline* (University Park: Pennsylvania State University Press, 1975).

24. Radhakrishnan, *Sourcebook,* 454.

25. Jacob Neusner, *Torah: From Scroll to Symbol in Formative Judaism* (Philadelphia: Fortress Press, 1985).

26. Ruqaiyyah Maqsood, *Islam* (London: Hodder, 1994), 29.

27. Ignatius Loyola, *Spiritual Exercises,* ed. Anthony Mottola (New York: Image Books, 1964), 13.

In Contrast to Sentimentality: Buddhist and Christian Sobriety

BARDWELL SMITH

Carleton College

A N INVITATION TO REFLECT on the spiritual disciplines of another tradition is a welcome but difficult assignment. It is welcome because having studied, taught about, and engaged in various forms of Buddhist practice for forty years, I have learned more about what becoming a Christian means than I had anticipated. So much so that I'm tempted to wonder, in Chuang Tzu style, am I a Buddhist-Christian, a Christian-Buddhist, or just another person for whom labels don't suffice? It is difficult because spiritual practice, by exhuming the most elusive levels of human experience, teaches one that the inner life resists all attempts to define, let alone control — which is a good thing, for the more claims made about one's practice, the more self-deception thrives.

The one claim I would make about my experiences of Buddhist spiritual practice, through meditation and pilgrimage, is that they have aroused immense gratitude for the fragile gift of life, plus a healthy respect for Buddhism's "three poisons of anger, greed, and ignorance," for they prod us to realize our essential nature. The same is true about the inner life of a Christian, which is why I said "becoming a Christian," for it is a process of unfoldment, not something static or accomplished. In other words, understanding the obstacles to spiritual growth within oneself, yet keeping one's eye on the potential that already exists in one's makeup (the buddha nature, the interdependence of all reality, or the image of god), helps one to persist without seeming to "progress" toward fulfilling this goal.

This essay is a personal reflection; it does not attempt to be academic. The learner-seeker in me seeks to become one with what he is teaching-seeking. While teaching himself, he is always being taught by others in the reciprocity of life. Having "forgotten" his essential nature, he seeks to "remember," to become what he already is, painfully aware that he is often living a contradiction. As one talks about spiritual practice, the reference is typically to some activity set apart from ordinary life. Actually, in such practice one seeks to impart greater candor and depth to one's everyday existence through some sort of spiritual discipline, in particular by the act of attending to life through conscious awareness. And though one's inner life resists all tendencies to impose order upon it, discipline can forge channels through which new life breathes.

Before discussing forms of Buddhist practice that have made an impact upon me, it makes sense to note some influences that came earlier and have remained indelible. Combat experience in the Marine Corps, compounded by exposure in North China in 1945–46 to kinds of suffering I had never imagined, prompted me to see the world and myself from a very different angle. In succeeding years Augustinian, Kierkegaardian, and Niebuhrian reflections on man's capacity for evil and self-deception taught me to regard claims to virtue or innocence with suspicion, to say the least. These were made especially graphic by portrayals of human brutality embodied in the worlds of a Dostoevsky or a Faulkner. When first exposed to Buddhist worldviews at the age of thirty-five, I found a comparable absence of sentimentality. Here too was a compelling awareness of the roots of suffering within each person and as magnified in social institutions and values. It was an awareness and acceptance of violence, evil, and self-deception as an inextricable part of the human experience; of greed, ignorance, anger, and hatred as threads in the tapestry of the human condition, but that a doorway out of this chamber of suffering also exists.

In the varieties of Christianity and Buddhism that fed my imagination, I found sober realism coexisting with profound belief in the human capacity for transformation. While Christians and Buddhists depict this tension in their own ways, I detect no basic disagreement. The disease of ignorance and of suffering is life-threatening, as we say, but the possibility for healing is immeasurable. The first step is the last step. Realizing that there is no selfhood except through our relationships constitutes the path to genuine freedom. Having had H. Richard Niebuhr as a teacher over many years, when I first encountered Buddhist visions of the interdependence of all reality, it was not difficult to see them as correlative with biblical metaphors about the kingdom of God. Whatever obscures this insight within oneself is not to be minimized but rather becomes grist for the mill of spiritual practice, as Shunryu Suzuki made clear in his teaching.[1] They are "mind weeds" that become compost for enriched practice and transformed life. Without awareness of obstacles within ourselves to this transformation, there are no breakthroughs in understanding, no paths to the healing of suffering.

It is the power of contrasting visions of the human condition — that is, suffering caused by attachment and liberation based upon a reality already present in the human potential for wholeness — that provides spiritual discipline its energy and direction. Vivid examples of these contrasting visions may be seen, among other places, in Dante's *Divine Comedy* or in the early Pali text, the Dhammapada. Through efforts in practicing this elusive yet inescapable wholeness, one comes to see and to recognize what prevents it from flowering and is thus helped to endure frustration without becoming dispirited. While it was not automatic for me to move from intellectual awareness of this reality to attempts to realize and practice it, I eventually found it to be a natural and unavoidable step toward authentic being. I am writing, therefore, from the perspective of one who alongside his teaching has sought to engage with others (students, faculty, and staff) on a number of occasions in meditation and in pilgrimage.

It is the nature of spiritual practice that the less abstract and more experiential it becomes, the more meaning we can discover within our daily life. By facing areas where we are especially vulnerable and by practicing the potential for wholeness in the midst of experiencing fragmentation, one bumps into new possibilities. But to put it this way is still abstract, for it is not a matter of the thinking mind. It is an awakening of the spirit to its inseparability from all other beings.

PILGRIMAGE AS SPIRITUAL PRACTICE

ON FREQUENT OCCASIONS in Japan, it has been on walking Buddhist pilgrimages on the island of Shikoku with groups of friends, colleagues, and students that I have treasured the most specific of experiences. These are the kind that lift one out of the usual pattern of one's daily routine and open one up to the unexpected and the freshness of unfolding life. They also provide insight into oneself, one's fellow pilgrims, and the ordinary Japanese folk whom one meets walking through the countryside, along mountain paths, and within the small rural towns and large cities of that lovely island. It is the testimony of most pilgrimage journals around the world that a major part of what is derived from such experience lies in the camaraderie and uncommon openness that characterize the way of the pilgrim. Victor Turner used the term *communitas* for this. Even though the sensation is transitory, it is genuine. In fact, its ephemerality is a powerful commentary about the difficulty of sustaining community in complex, conflicted, and ever changing circumstances. The pilgrim's experience provides a modest vision, a taste of alternatives to mistrust and bias. Its very uncommonness is the other side of the dual vision mentioned above. Rather than ruing its passing as one returns to one's daily routine, one is led to wonder more about what constitutes authentic community. However briefly savored, one's hunger for extended forms of justice, peace, and kindness in our communal life and body politic is increased.

As one learns more about one's own religion and culture through studying those of another, and learns more about oneself by seeing oneself reflected in the other, it is by walking an ancient pilgrimage path (*henro michi*), as on Shikoku, that a richer sense of history, legend, myth, and symbol has made its steady impact on me. Richard Niebuhr talked of becoming "contemporaneous" with other figures and times in Christian history.[2] It is my experience that through pilgrimage this sensing of kinship with a different approach to life and thought is enlivened. While one can study about another religious tradition from afar, one learns from within onself as one takes the time to experience tradition in slow motion, step after step. Each temple one visits or stays at, each cluster of fellow pilgrims one meets and talks with, each expression of iconography or constructed tradition is different and affects one differently. In the process, one experiences the uniqueness and freshness of each moment, relieved for a spell from conditioned, unconscious responses to preset, daily routines.

Inevitably, one compares this temple and that setting with others on this circular web that connects and distinguishes the "eighty-eight" pilgrimage temples of Shikoku from each other. All along this thousand-mile path, which one trods in small or long portions for days or weeks, the mind travels in its own directions, and one thinks of other journeys one has taken or may yet take. The mind's pilgrimage is a constant process; its main arresting spots occur in one form of meditation or another. One's memory locates experiences within a larger fabric whose threads represent unpredictable but significant relationships. On my most recent Shikoku journey, one that extended for four weeks in the autumn of 1996, I found myself juxtaposing aspects of Buddhism with parallel ingredients in Christian life and thought. In discussing these thoughts with colleagues on this pilgrimage (some of whom were Buddhist, some Christian, and some with no religious leaning), we had a sense of polishing each other's appreciation of what we were doing. The metaphor that came to mind was the familiar one of apprentice monks (*unsui*) in a Zen monastery who serve as diamonds polishing each other's experience in ways that make uniqueness shine more brightly in a communal setting than when alone.

As one seeks to practice the pilgrim's path from another tradition (whether Christian or Buddhist), one discovers what one could never imagine before. It was only three years later, in September 1999, that four of us who had walked together on Shikoku were part of a larger pilgrim group on the path (*camino*) to Santiago in northern Spain. Since none of us was Roman Catholic, this path was initially as foreign to us as some Christians may have felt about the Buddhist path on Shikoku. As one participates in the specific forms of another's tradition, it does not take long to become part of some larger human pilgrimage. In this experience there is a process of instantaneous translation from one symbol system to another, which is in no sense a scrambling of metaphors or ritual expression. It is, instead, similar to what Buddhist monks in Sri Lanka and Thailand felt instinctively when they met Thomas Merton, as he did with them. It was a resonance in the reciprocity of being. It was the quality of respecting each other and being transformed by the meeting. The openness that exists in such meetings is as unforced as the opening of a flower to the warmth of sunlight.

In this sense, what we felt in the packed cathedral in Santiago in the presence of fervently believing Spanish pilgrims was analogous to experiencing in quite ordinary temples on Shikoku the very different expressions of Buddhist reverence for the bodhisattva Kannon or for Kōbō Daishi, the great Shingon saint and savior figure. The faith expressed in these significantly diverse forms of practice was neither culturally nor personally our own, though it summoned from us at quite profound levels the same capacity for faith and for seeing the oneness behind the many. It was, in other words, a stretching of the spirit, and thus became part of one's own uncharted spiritual journey.[3]

MEDITATION AS SPIRITUAL PRACTICE

OVER THE PAST thirty years, it has been my privilege to engage in meditative practice with students, faculty, and colleagues of various backgrounds. The settings for such practice have varied from Anglican and Catholic monasteries, Protestant churches, Quaker meeting places, and various sites on college campuses to Buddhist meditation centers in this country as well as Sötö and Rinzai temples in Japan. Small groups of communal meditative practice have occurred recently at the UCC Church in Northfield, Minnesota, under my supervision over periods of several weeks. And for ten weeks each, daily sessions of Buddhist meditation have been conducted at Carleton College under the direction of Eshin Nishimura, a Rinzai priest and scholar from Kyoto, first in 1971 and again in 1989; of Dhiravamsa, a Thai meditation master, in 1975; and in the early 1980s of Dainin Katagiri Roshi, the late head of the Minnesota Zen Center.

In none of these four occasions was doctrine a primary point of focus, though forms of Christian or Buddhist teachings were used for illustrative purposes. The emphasis was on developing deeper levels of mindfulness, of paying attention to the untidy nature of one's conscious and subconscious thinking and emotions. The experience of those participating ranged from those who had never done meditation before to those who had practiced one form of sitting or another for years. Despite this variance, the primary advice for such practice was not to dwell on one's past experience nor on what the future may hold, but to practice again and again the "beginner's mind," to experience life with freshness, to put aside prior thoughts and preconceptions.[4] The practice of sitting quietly, being mindful about the thoughts and feelings that rise to the surface and practicing the ability of letting them go in the same fashion as breathing in and breathing out is, as every "meditator" knows, easier said than done. Becoming a "beginner" when one is not a beginner is both a lure and a peril, for it means contending with forms of self-recognition that are either unfamiliar or all too familiar.

If one meditates without guidance, discouragement is inevitable. Even with guidance, discouragement is inevitable but can be used as part of a process that sees "negative experience" as having purposes one cannot always understand and thus finds difficult to tolerate. By observing oneself and learning about the experiences of others, one finds that while the results one might have hoped for are elusive, the consequence of pursuing such practice beyond discouragement leads to indirect results one could not have predicted. The main point is that one is to meditate without motivation. This disconnect between expectations and actual experience is the inevitable no-man's land, which requires guidance from another if one is to persevere. While each person's experience in these ten-week sessions under a meditation master varied considerably, there was remarkable consensus at the conclusion about how focused the rest of their life had, at least temporarily, become — academic work, personal relations, sense of time, knowledge about themselves, and more. The discipline of looking within, of attending to with care and attention, was reflected in other threads of the tapestry of one's life. In a fundamental sense, the whole universe becomes one's teacher.

If none of this was necessarily "Buddhist," there was the recognition by those who had grown up in another religious tradition, or in none, that there was an important link between teaching and practice that was not common in their experience before. As both traditions stress, it is practice and experience that give import to teaching. In Katagiri Roshi's words, it is life that gives birth to thought, not thought to life. For Christians who still value their own tradition but do not find adequate attention given to spiritual discipline within nonmonastic Christian circles, the sense of appreciation can be enormous, as in my own case. Paradoxically, with cumulative practice I felt a deepening of spiritual hunger and that this hunger was healthy and appropriate. It was not a hunger for what I did not have, but a hunger for what I truly am yet have not nearly become. While I recognized the importance of meditative practice in many monastic traditions in the West — and for me the Benedictine was the most compelling — what Buddhist meditation had to offer was a spiritual discipline that required neither a monastic setting nor credal acceptance. It requires only the meditator. With a taste for the real, one is no longer willing to settle for what is illusion.

Obviously, there have been increasing numbers of Christians, initially from monastic backgrounds, who have found Buddhist meditation to be deeply nurturing to their own spiritual growth. Considering the fact that Christians and

Buddhists have only been sharing and practicing each other's meditative disciplines for the past few decades, it is no wonder that labels cannot suffice for what they are in the process of becoming. As fellow members of the one human family, they are sustained by returning to the one immeasurable ground of being in overlapping ways. Whatever this sharing will become, labels will never do it justice. And for most of us these days, meditation not only helps us to encounter the untidy elements of our inner life, but to be engaged with issues in society with greater wisdom, compassion, kindness, and perhaps even some humility.

Notes

1. *Zen Mind, Beginner's Mind* (New York and Tokyo: Weatherhill, 1970), 32–33. One finds this notion persistent in the writings of Dôgen Zenji, the founder of Sôtô Zen.

2. H. Richard Niebuhr, *Christ and Culture* (New York: Harper & Brothers, 1951), 248–49.

3. If the point of this essay were a comparative look at pilgrimage, it would make sense to write more about the Santiago experience. This may happen at some other time. The point here is merely to indicate, however briefly, that folk from one tradition may be deeply moved by participating as a pilgrim at the sacred sites of another tradition.

4. This is the basic theme of *Zen Mind, Beginner's Mind.*

BUDDHIST RESPONSES

A Buddhist Reflects (Practices Reflection) on Some Christians' Reflections on Buddhist Practices

GRACE BURFORD
Prescott College

A tourist lost in New York City asks of a passerby, "How do I get to Carnegie Hall?" The musically inclined informant replies, "Practice, practice, practice!"

OFTEN PEOPLE WHO have just heard I am a college professor with a specialty in Buddhism ask me "Are you a practicing Buddhist?" This question has always stumped me. My most common retort (it's not really an answer), "I keep practicing; maybe someday I'll get it right," both evades and critiques the question. As we use the term in everyday conversation, "practice" generally means disciplined repetition of an activity, usually in preparation for a performance of some kind. In relation to a religious path, "practice" usually refers to the integration of certain prescribed actions (practices) in one's life. My retort derives from the mixing of these two meanings of the word "practice," and the assumption that — for one reason or another — religious practice does not lead to a perfect performance in the spiritual equivalent of Carnegie Hall.

The form of the question puzzles me. Why do they ask about my practice? Why not just ask me "Are you a Buddhist?" I think they expect to discover that I engage in a Buddhist equivalent of going to church. Maybe the inclusion of practice in the question indicates anticipation of some level of earnestness, of application of my self/energy/time in service of my religion — some outward, observable manifestation of my religious orientation, above and beyond just teaching college students about this religion. Perhaps they expect me to confess to being a vegetarian, or meditating, or chanting, or attending Buddhist services of some kind. Although I find the question somewhat intrusive, I understand that most often it arises from well-meaning curiosity, if not genuine interest, and I try to follow my retort with something more pedagogically effective.

For most of my life, practice has been about music. I sang before I talked; I began to study piano at an early age; in elementary school I took up guitar and clarinet; in high school I started voice lessons. Learning to play all of these instruments required practice. Recently, I took up the electric bass guitar, and I'm back to daily practicing. Practice does produce something; it is linearly causal. If I practice my instrument, I get better at producing the sounds I want to produce. Only a nonmusician would say this does not amount to a real accomplishment. At the same time, the activity one practices is the same activity one hopes to perform: I play the bass when I practice, in order to be able to play the bass. Still, I must practice — to get where I want to go, to improve the quality of my playing. After all, I first heard the Carnegie Hall joke from my guitar teacher, who told it both to amuse me *and* to inspire me to practice, practice, practice. At about the same time, author Catherine Drinker Bowen advised a group of us high school students that — based on her experiences growing up in a family full of musicians — the most effective way to learn an instrument is to fall in love with one's music teacher. In other words, desire serves the crucial function of inspiring one to practice. Yet I know that the same desire that motivates me to practice so that I can play more skillfully (as in "practice makes perfect") can hold me back if I focus on that future desired skillful playing (the "perfection") instead of the present moment of my playing. Further, I can practice to the point of technical expertise — I can accomplish that skill level I am aiming for in practice — and still not produce the musical quality I aspire to play. Practice does produce something necessary, but that something does not suffice. Musicians are no better at naming that other necessary ingredient than are mystics, but we recognize its presence or absence immediately, whether in ourselves or others. As a senior in high school, I saw that I often met it in singing, seldom at the piano, and almost never with a clarinet. So I decided to focus my classical music study on developing my voice.

How does musical practice relate to spiritual practice? I find some overlap in the disciplined structure of both, as well as in the universal importance of remembering to breathe whether one is singing or playing bass, practicing or performing, meditating or chanting. Like musical practice, spiritual practice hones skills, including the religiously valued abilities to do one thing (e.g., sit) for a long time; to focus on one object or idea; to breathe freely; to suspend our rush to judgment; to love; to be loved; to act out of compassion; to see things as they really are; to love our neighbors as ourselves; to do everything we do with full attention. In spiritual life, as in music, practice hones the necessary technical skills and opens one up to meet that other crucial component at once so hard to name and so easily recognized. Christians might call that component "grace"; Buddhists tend to resist the naming, although the combination of wisdom and compassion might point to it.

What is the relationship between practice and performance? Although I have often performed music in public, I suffer from stage fright to an extent others find surprising. Stage fright prevents me from performing to the best of my musical ability and prevents me from enjoying performance. Once I took a workshop on stage fright prevention that was being offered at the music school where I was studying voice. The message of that entire workshop boiled down to this: the best, in fact the only, way to counter stage fright is to practice, practice, practice. Like stage fright, fear in general can undermine our full presence in life and thereby keep us from living to the best of our abilities and from enjoying life. I suspect that spiritual practice may constitute the best, if not the only, way to counter life fright.

What is Buddhist practice? Is it different from Buddhist practices? Can we separate Buddhist practices from "being Buddhist"? Why do people ask me if I'm a practicing Buddhist, but they don't ask me if I'm a practicing musician? Do they assume a musician, to be a musician, must practice, but one can be a Buddhist without practicing? Typically, Buddhists practice to realize that none of what we do is practice. The paradox lies in the fact that knowing this does not constitute a shortcut; we still must practice to realize that there is no difference between practice and performance. The factor that makes a difference to us, that is, how well we are doing it (in this case, living), actually does *make* the difference. When we do it (i.e., live) well, the difference turns out to have no substance. Still, we must practice in order to realize that nondifference, to get from making the difference to not making the difference, from practicing in the home studio to performing in Carnegie Hall. Around and around we go. As the Christians who reflect here on Buddhist practice observe, this sort of talk emerges from trying to capture practice in propositions. Nevertheless, I will carry on.

Two assumptions underlie these five essays: the authors are Christians, and they have had some kind of meaningful encounters with Buddhist practices. By my tally, they say they have gained from these encounters three types of benefits. First, they have found confirmation of things they already knew from their engagement with Christianity and alternate forms of practices they were already engaged in as Christians. Second, they have learned some other things they could have learned from Christianity but had not. Terry Muck, Paul Ingram, and Bardwell Smith address this second type of benefit most explicitly. In all three cases, this type of benefit from their encounters with Buddhist practice derives primarily from the fact that Buddhism was for them an "other" religion rather than from anything unique to Buddhism. Third, the authors have picked up a few things they could not have learned from Christianity, things particular to Buddhism. Specifically, they reflect on uniquely Buddhist practice techniques, such as silent sitting (with or without purpose), mindfulness-awareness meditation, mental concentration or focus, and the general level of mental and physical rigor of Buddhist meditative practice. They interpret these practices in self-consciously Christian terms and value them as alternative ways to accomplish Christian goals, but they identify the practices themselves as distinctively Buddhist.

When (most of) the authors identify themselves as Christian and describe certain practices they engage in as distinctively Buddhist, they go along with the assumption underlying their assigned task; namely, we can mix distinct religious identity (Christian) with practice techniques associated with another religion (Buddhism) without compromising the religious specificity of either the identities (Christian) or the techniques (Buddhist). The techniques, it turns out, can also be separated from their experienced results, or — more precisely — from the interpretations of those experiences. The practitioners can be Christians, the techniques Buddhist, and the resulting experiences interpreted along Christian lines. This makes sense to me. The techniques have to come from somewhere, and to call them Buddhist amounts to acknowledging that Buddhists came up with them in the context of Buddhist beliefs and Buddhist interpretations of experiences. Interpretations of religious experience, being propositional, fit into the propositional schemes we call religious doctrines. These tend to exclude each other, which is what makes religions different from each other, so both the techniques and the interpretations of the experiences they give rise to can be Buddhist or Christian. Identity too seems to be an exclusive affair, naming what we are (Christian or Buddhist) with reference to what we are not (Buddhist or Christian) and choosing allegiances in terms of propositions (God, Dharmakaya). As several of these authors indicate, the experiences themselves defy dualistic categorization (which clarifies their — and my — position within the ongoing and often heated debate about whether we ever experience anything outside our interpretive categories); but both the religious identities of the experiencers and their interpretation of the experiences belong in the realm of dualistic thinking.

So a Christian can engage in a Buddhist practice, gain from it something meaningful in Christian terms, and remain a Christian. As a (practicing) Buddhist, I might quibble with the claim that these practices remain Buddhist, even when Christians modify them to suit their purposes, when they impose on them conceptual frameworks and interpretations that fly in the face of basic Buddhist interpretations of the nature of reality. Honestly, I cannot get excited about this argument, perhaps because I think the distinctively Buddhist nature of these practices matters very little to the Christians who practice them. They like these practices because they work for them, not because they are Buddhist practices, per se. Similarly, participation in the production of glorious Christian music (the Gabrieli *Magnificat a 12,* Vivaldi's *Gloria,* the Bach *B Minor Mass,* Beethoven's *Ninth Symphony,* the Verdi *Requiem,* Rachmaninov's *Vespers,* and oh-so-many more) has enriched my life immeasurably, but to my mind this benefit comes despite, rather than because of, the music's Christian content and inspiration. In an even closer parallel to the experiences presented in these five essays, these days I strive to practice observance of the Sabbath as a day of rest, because it works for me — it nourishes my spiritual life — not because it is a Jewish (and Christian) practice.

I am willing to agree to disagree with Christians about how to interpret the experiences that arise from applications of Buddhist practices, because at least these five Christians demonstrate that Buddhist practices have enriched their spiritual lives in ways that mean far more to the world than would any dualistic, rational propositions. For Bardwell Smith, engagement with Buddhist practices have "aroused immense gratitude for the fragile gift of life" and respect for "anger, greed, and ignorance." Smith also names increased meaning in daily life; a "stretching of the spirit"; and a deepening of his "spiritual hunger" as products of this encounter. Paul Ingram acknowledges two lessons he learned from "interior dialogue with Buddhists," concerning the paths of our inward journeys and the difference between experiences and propositions. Mary Frohlich values primarily the rigor of Buddhist meditative practice and finds support for Christian "unknowing" in the Zen Buddhist notion of "don't know mind." Frances Adeney finds that the Buddhist practice of silent sitting fosters self-understanding, helps her let go of attachments, and deepens her "connection with the depths of Life." Terry Muck learned from his study of Buddhism the deeply significant "lesson of readiness." Many of these authors also mention that their engagement with Buddhist practices has led them "to be engaged with issues in society with greater wisdom, compassion, kindness, and perhaps even some humility" (Smith); to "experience the suffering of others as our suffering...and the liberation of others as our liberation—and thereby we become empowered for social engagement" (Ingram); "to extend compassion to others who are hurt or oppressed" (Adeney).

In the realm of exclusive religious identities, of beliefs and techniques and interpretations of experience, you are either in a different group, or you are in my group. Either you focus your meditation on Christ, or you don't; you assume the grace of God, or you don't. But in the realm of action in this world, our interpretations need not divide us. What these authors get out of doing Buddhist practice need not be conversion to Buddhism to be beneficial to Buddhists as well as to Christians, and everyone else, for that matter. If Buddhist practices help Christians act for the greater good, as the reports of these Christians indicate they do, then regardless of the labels we put on the people or their practices, the results make the world a better place for us all. So—speaking as a Buddhist and as an inhabitant of the web of life—to Christians who want to adopt Buddhist practices the way these Christians have done, I say (along with every music teacher I have ever had) practice, practice, practice!

Christian Experiences with Buddhist Spirituality: A Response

ROBERT THURMAN

Columbia University

RECENTLY I READ an account on the CNN website of a statement made at the Kumbh Mela at Allahabad in India, where about eighty million devotees of Hinduism were joined in their worship of the grace of the Goddess River Ganga by His Holiness the Dalai Lama, informal head of Tibetan Buddhists and formal head of the Tibetan government in exile. His Holiness also joined the leaders of Hinduism, various Shankaracharyas and others, in a formal statement in which they requested with the followers of other world religions not to persist in the practice of aggressive conversion of the followers of other religions. The statement addressed a special plea to Christians and Muslims, who may currently be the most intense in their worldwide missionary activities.

The writer of the CNN article was clearly cynical about this, mentioning, as if to undercut the force of their appeal to other religions, that the Hindu leaders themselves wanted to declare India a Hindu nation. He noted that the Dalai Lama "giggled" when he sprinkled himself with Ganga water out of respect for Hindu beliefs, but declined to immerse himself in the river, saying it was too cold.

His Holiness has often challenged leaders of world religions, including Buddhists, Hindus, and secular humanists (which he considers a world religion/ideology, whether Marxist or liberal democratic), by saying that now is past the time when anyone should be attempting to convert others to a different belief system or institutional affiliation. If persisted in, it will lead to worse violence in the future than it already has in the past. His position seems eminently reasonable, looking realistically at the world situation, the powerful technologies of communication and possible scale of violence. Yet people filled with enthusiasm for their saving faith tend to feel deprived if they cannot have a mission to save others with it.

I do not think His Holiness means that you cannot share your enthusiasm, or make the jewels of faith, wisdom, and compassion of your tradition accessible to others, or even dialogue with others comparing your tradition with theirs. He travels the world teaching Buddhism, mostly to Buddhists, but freely to anyone who is interested. But then he does tell those who are not Buddhists *not* to convert to Buddhism. Rather, he cautions, they should take whatever they learn and use anything that seems good to them to enhance their original tradition, thereby remaining integrated with their families, communities, and local customs, perhaps even enriching their own traditions. Those who are Buddhists from birth he urges to study other traditions, learn from them, and critically extricate themselves from feelings of superiority or estrangement. And some who may already have chosen to become Buddhist he strongly cautions not to criticize their birth traditions or look down on their followers.

What I love about the essays in this collection is that they all seem to be learning from Buddhism and appreciate its traditions, yet they interpret it in Christian terms, apply it to their own Christian understanding, and practice an enriched Christianity, perhaps what Bardwell Smith so aptly calls in his essay "becoming a Christian." I feel privileged to respond to the deep personal quest for truth I sense within each essay. I am not going to review each essay point by point, though I will touch on each of the five as I follow a kind of pilgrimage through them. Though all five essays are personal and confessional, those by Ingram and Muck are perhaps more theoretical in tone, Adeney and Frohlich more contemplative in focus, and Smith combines both in a special combination I will save for last.

Paul Ingram writes as a man who floats contentedly in a sea of God's grace, the vision of which seems to have been opened for him by Martin Luther. While he floats, he reflects deeply and knowledgeably about both Pure Land and Zen Buddhisms, acknowledging how his appreciation of the Christian life has been enriched by the pluralistic encounter with these traditions. He seems to assume that the ultimate interdependence of all things is similarly taught by both Buddhism (*pratityasamutpada*) and Christianity (doctrines of creation and incarnation — here one wonders where the austere "absolute otherness of God" has gone). The only "disagreement" he seems to find is a Buddhist tendency not to consider things to be as "drenched with feelings" as in his oceanic world of grace. He makes a good point that practice should not be instrumentalized in either tradition, as it is ultimately nondual with attainment, and he elucidates his own Buddhicized Christianity in terms of theoretical reflection, centering prayer, and social engagement.

Terry Muck has learned a lot about Theravada Buddhism in a deep way, and he illustrates the value of interreligious dialogue by telling us his journey of discovery of something crucial about Christianity that he was directed to by Buddhism. In looking into the key concept of "readiness" for the spiritual path, trying to understand what it consists of and how one comes to it, he noticed while studying Buddhism that morality (*sila*) is considered foundational for the path, is tantamount to readiness, unpacked as possession of faith or confidence (*saddha*) and enterprise, or creative effort (*viriya*). He then noted that in his understanding of Christianity, morality was the fruit of the spiritual path, not the foundation. Spurred by this apparent dissonance between the traditions, he explored both of them more deeply and discovered that morality is both foundation and result, both seed and flower, in both traditions. This illustrates for him the value of interreligious encounter, that confronting of dissonance can lead to a deeper understanding of living resonance. His concluding scheme of the "dynamics of readiness" is a useful deployment of the four noble truths in the context of the Christian path to salvation.

Frances Adeney generously shares her story of Buddhist-Christian interweaving, explaining how she came to write a Christian haiku poem:

> The frog
> sat
> On the lily pad
> Not waiting.

She tells of a long experience of silent meditation from within the Christian context of personal relationship to God through Christ. When she discovered a Buddhist approach, it was from the teaching of a German Trappist monk who lived in a monastery in Indonesia! What was Buddhist about it was that the silence was not God-focused, immersion was not scripture-based, and the contemplation process was without objectified goal (here she assumes that Buddhism is universally impersonal, transverbal, and focused on the moment — not necessarily so, but it is not important in this vivid essay). Practicing "entering the silence" in this way, she found it immensely helpful in her spiritual life at that time. She concludes by saying that a Christian can employ such Buddhist practice most fruitfully as (1) preparation for encounter with God, (2) a way of fostering deeper self-understanding, and (3) a discipline for losing the petty self in the divine vastness. The frog is released on the lily pad by not having to wait any further. Her last statement is memorable, "silence does not belong to Buddhism or any other tradition — we belong to it."

Mary Frohlich explores the famous Zen "don't know mind," the orientation of radical openness to reality rid of ego-manipulation, and compares it with the Cloud of Unknowing contemplative discipline of Christian mysticism. She makes the important statement in this context that in the modern world it is impossible to maintain any sort of "pure" "insertion in a single tradition," and that adherence even to the tradition one is born in reflects choices and ideas that are significantly marked by the pluralistic presence of other traditions. Most interestingly, she shares her own daily practice of Christian contemplation, wherein she does *lectio divina* in the morning and less structured immersion in the presence of Christ in the evening — both sessions using a Zen *zafu* meditation pillow and Indian yogic lotus sitting posture. She needlessly worries about Buddhist meditations being filled with "spirits," which she recognizes in the struggles of the Christian desert fathers and thinks might be a serious difference — having been misled by a reviewer's offhand comment based on the stereotype of traditional/modern. (Buddhist meditation sciences are quite alert to possible distractions by spirits and are adept at avoiding them.) She then beautifully describes her most precious moments of abandoned trust in Christ, which she "don't knowingly" speculates share in the liberation of "don't know mind" of the Zen tradition.

Bardwell Smith's reflections in a way preempt all my reactions and crown this fascinating collection. He purports to go beyond spiritual sentimentality in either tradition and bring them into encounter in a spirit of sobriety, yet his combination of reflective maturity, contemplative discipline, and personal pilgrimage touches inner chords that are certainly moving, albeit soberly. He confesses right away that he has done so much Buddhist Christian dialogue that he is like Chuang Tzu, who so vividly dreamed he was a butterfly that he ever after said he could never be sure if he was a man who dreamed he was a butterfly or a butterfly dreaming he is a man. Smith says "having studied, taught about, and engaged in various forms of Buddhist practice for forty years, I have learned more about what becoming a Christian means than I anticipated." I would like to quote in full the following paragraph, which says everything I would like to say about what Buddhist-Christian dialogue can do for either Buddhist or Christian as they try to become what they truly are; however, I don't have to since you can turn back in this collection and reread that paragraph yourself. Smith also shares with us his profoundly formative experience as a Marine in the Great War, his obviously shattering disillusionment about human nature as he encountered the brutality, the degradation, the inhuman capacity for cruelty and evil. This then sets the themes of dialogue, pilgrimage, and meditation against the strong commitment not to gloss over these harsh realities as we seek to unfold the Christ nature or the Buddha nature. It is more remarkable then that he finds sustenance in both traditions, in their basic agreement about life, that there is a way to overcome the dark side. He most pithily says that both traditions agree that the realization that there is no selfhood apart from through relationships is the path to genuine freedom. That practice leads to deepening of this experience.

In his description of his experiences of pilgrimage, the eighty-eight-temple circuit on Buddhist Shikoku Island and the Santiago de Compostela pilgrimage in Catholic Spain, he makes me think of the Dalai Lama's love of going on multifaith pilgrimages, asking Hindus and Muslims to join him at Buddhist holy places, going with them to their holy places, and inviting them to join him in visiting Jerusalem and Rome and Lourdes. The breaking of routines, the formation of *communitas* in a sacred setting that is grounded in but transcends proprietarial identity, Smith describes all of this so well. In his last section on meditation, he says

For Christians who still value their own tradition but do not find adequate attention given to spiritual discipline within nonmonastic Christian circles, the sense of appreciation can be enormous, as in my own case. Paradoxically, with cumulative practice I felt a deepening of spiritual hunger and that this hunger was healthy and appropriate. It was not a hunger for what I did not have, but a hunger for what I truly am yet have not nearly become... what Buddhist meditation had to offer was a spiritual discipline that neither required a monastic setting nor credal acceptance. It requires only the meditator. With a taste for the real, one is no longer willing to settle for what is illusion.

In the spirit of Smith's generous statement, any Buddhist can learn from dialogue with Christianity or another tradition that it is more a matter of living in the spirit of "becoming a Buddhist" than some fixed state of "being a Buddhist." If religions can make themselves felt from this angle, they can make a critical contribution in his postmodern time of universal insecurity about identity in helping people rise above the lethal tendency of the hardening of identities and discover in pluralism an unprecedented opportunity to live more meaningfully.

CHRISTIAN SPIRITUAL PRACTICE
AS SEEN BY BUDDHISTS

Formal Practice:
Buddhist or Christian

Robert Aitken

Diamond Sangha

In this paper, I write from a Mahayana perspective and take up seven Buddhist practices and the views that bring them into being, together with Christian practices that may be analogous, in turn with their inspiration. The Buddhist practices sometimes tend to blend and take on another's attributes and functions. I name them according to their usage in Western Buddhism.

1. The *Nembutsu* (Ch. *Nien-fo,* "Recalling Buddha") is the pronouncement of veneration to Amida Butsu (Ch. *A-mi-to-fo,* Skt. *Amitabha Buddha*), an appeal to his salvific power, and sometimes an endeavor to unify with him.

2. The *ekomon* (Ch. *hui-hsiang-men,* Skt. *parinamana*) is a verse that transfers merit back to Buddhas, bodhisattvas, and past teachers for their further empowerment to bring beings to the way of the Buddha.

3. *Zazen* (Ch. *tsao-ch'an,* Skt. *dhyana*) is focused meditation intended to enable the student to personalize the realization and way of the Buddha.

4. The vow or expression of aspiration (J. *gan,* Ch. *yuan,* Skt. *pranidhana*) pronounces a determination to make realization possible for the self and others.

5. *Sange,* or *zange* (Ch. *chang-hui,* Skt. *kshamayati*), is the confession of personal responsibility for bad karma in the past and repentance for it.

6. *Mudra* (J. *in,* Ch. *yin*) and *dharani* (J. *darani* or *ju,* Ch. *chou*) are ritualized presentations of realizations and their dharma. They can be gestures, hand positions, or postures; *dharani* are esoteric formulas or texts.

7. Sutras and sutra services, from the Sanskrit (J. *kyo,* Ch. *ching*), traditional Buddhist chants and texts.

THE NEMBUTSU

THE NEMBUTSU invokes Amida, the Buddha of Infinite Light and Life and the Lord of the Pure Land, a powerful savior by dint of vows he took while still in his Bodhisattva Dharmakara incarnation. He is venerated across Asia — in Japan, Korea, Vietnam, and the Chinese diaspora. The Nembutsu formula, *"Namu amida butsu,"* or the equivalent in the other languages ("Veneration to 'Amida Butsu'"), is repeated devotionally, bringing promise of a joyous afterlife, and for some, intimacy with Amida, the spiritual *oyasama,* or parent, an effect not unlike that of Christian mysticism.[1] The Myokonin (Pure and Happy People), the Pure Land movement of Japanese who take it upon themselves to practice the Nembutsu moment-to-moment, set forth their experience in artless poetry that is poignant and metaphysically clear:

> I thought it was all due to my self-power,
> That [the Nembutsu] was uttered;
> But it was not so, it all came from the power of Oya.
> What I was imagining to be the other power
> Was no other than the self-power itself.
> Wishing to shun the evil path
> And ever hoping for the Pure land —
> The very thought was no other than the self-power.
>
> I have been designing all the time,
> Saying, "Is this the way, or that?"
> But there was no designing after all,
> All was given fully, and freely
> How grateful I am! *Namu amida butsu!*[2]

Interior repetition of the Nembutsu hundreds of times a day brings the fulfilling gift of spiritual intimacy with the *oya*, and the Christian *analoy* is clearly the Jesus Prayer, "Lord Jesus Christ, Son of God, have mercy on me, a sinner," or its shortened version," Lord have mercy" (*"Kyrie eleison"*).[3] Yet there is more than a shade of difference between devotion to a savior empowered by his original vows for his all-embracing compassion, and devotion to the one who inherits the power of an omnipotent God. In the words of Saint Teresa of Avila, "God is almighty. His power has equaled His will; and so He can do everything that pleases him. The less I understand this, the more I believe it and the greater the devotion it arouses in me. Blessed is He forever! Amen."[4]

The *Ekomon*

In contrast to the Nembutsu, the *ekomon* is not an appeal for redemption but a return of the "auspicious power" (J. *fukutoku*, Ch. *fu-tu*, Skt. *punya*) of the sutra or sutras just recited to Buddhist ancestors and archetypal entities. Contemporary personages may also be beneficiaries. The auspicious power of those reciting the *ekomon*, accumulated through virtuous deeds, is also returned by the recitation.

The classical *sutta* does not close with an *ekomon*, but with an account of how well the Buddha's words were received by his disciples. The form emerges with the appearance of commentaries, such as Shantideva's *Bodhicaryavatara*, which has a lengthy *ekomon* that extends the merit he accumulated by composing his book to the afflicted and endangered of the world: "Through my merit may those in any of the directions find oceans of happiness and delight...."[5]

In contemporary usage the *ekomon* is tailored to the sutras it follows, and is often varied to fit the circumstances. In the Diamond Sangha, the ceremony of accepting the Buddhist precepts ends with an *ekomon* that evokes both kinds of auspicious power — from sutras, and from the *sangha* — in this case, after a *sesshin* or retreat:

> At Magadha, at this very place,
> deep into the sacred ground,
> high into the empty sky,

broadly shading living things
the tree of wisdom thrives
by rain and soil and sunshine
and by your loving care that we maintain.
We dedicate the *Prajnaparamita Heart Sutra,*
our ceremony of *Jukai,* our *sesshin,* and ourselves
to you, Great Founder Shakyamuni Buddha,
we celebrate your sacred presence,
your boundless understanding, and your love.
Let your true Dharma continue,
and your Sangha relations become complete;
    all Buddhas throughout space and time;
    all Bodhisattvas, Mahasattvas,
    the great *Prajnaparamita.*[6]

The *Jukai* (Ch. *Shou-chiai*) ceremony of accepting the precepts is an acknowledgement that the Buddha Shakyamuni is my teacher, and thus it is appropriate that the *ekomon* at its close be a dedication to him. "We tend your tree of wisdom with the loving care you have instilled in us, and return that auspicious power to you with celebration and gratitude." The traditional formula at the end of this *ekomon* extends *fukutoku* back to all Buddhas, Bodhisattvas, Mahasattvas (Great Beings), and to the perfection of wisdom itself, the *Prajnaparamita* — almost personified, like female images of *Prajna* venerated in the Vajrayana tradition. Sutras at other times will end with *ekomon* directed to specific Buddhas, Bodhisattvas, or past teachers — or to friends and members who are ill, or who have died.

Dana, the gift and its circulation, is the rationale of the *ekomon.* We send out whatever auspicious power we have accumulated, and by that act we are empowered further for our bodhisattva work.

Another kind of empowerment is concentrated in the *O-Daimoku,* the "August Title" of the Lotus Sutra, recited by Nichiren followers in the formula *"Namu myoho renge kyo,"* "Veneration to the *Subtle Dharma Lotus Sutra.*" For mainstream Nichiren Buddhists and their offspring in "new religions," this is an evocation of the Buddhist teaching of wisdom and "appropriate means" in the Lotus Sutra. It is considered to be a container of all Buddhist paths, the way to full religious realization, to union with a Buddha, and to rebirth in the Pure Land, and for the enlightenment of those who have died. Its use to foster world peace, to gain worldly benefits and even as a mantra for exorcism can be found among the new religions.[7]

These new religions include the Nipponzan Myohoji, whose monks chant the August Title as an *ekomon* for international, interethnic, and interreligious harmony. This purpose is the same as close devotions during Roman Catholic mass. With each supplication by the priest for friends who are ill, for those who have died, and for people across the world who are suffering tribulations, the congregation responds, "Lord, hear our prayer." The Myohoji chant evokes the compassion embedded in a sutra, the Christian prayer supplicates an omnipotent God, both for the sake of all beings.

Nowhere among Mahayana practices is concern for other beings expressed more clearly than in the *metta* practice of loving kindness in Theravada Buddhism. One begins with a focus upon the self:

> May I be free from danger.
> May I have mental happiness.
> May I have physical happiness.
> May I have the ease of well-being.[8]

Metta then is directed to those near and dear — may they be free from danger, and so on — then to those about whom one feels neutral, then to enemies, and so on to all beings. Under the guidance of a seasoned teacher, the resistance one feels to this compassionate practice is faced squarely and allowed to wither and disappear.

This way of *metta* is the first of the Four Noble Abodes of loving kindness, compassion, sympathetic joy, and equanimity. In the Theravada view, *metta* is the ground of the Noble Abodes,[9] as contrasted with the Zen view, which would probably name equanimity the ground.[10] In practice *metta* is another Buddhist devotion that is like the prayer for friends far and near in Roman Catholic mass, except that it begins with compassionate self-affirmation. The mainstream Catholic view that gives rise to "mea culpa" releases personal power to God. Yet outside this convention, self-affirmation is found in Liberation Theology, which empowers the oppressed with the realization that Jesus was a man of the poor,[11] and is also found in the preaching of Meister Eckhart and his

heirs: "People think God has only become a human being *there,* in his historical incarnation — but that is not so, for God is *here,* in this very place — just
as much incarnate a human being as long ago. And this is why he has become
incarnate as a human being: that he might give birth to you as his only begotten
Son, and no less."[12]

Some Mahayana *ekomon* appeal to other powers, and of special interest to
this study is the memorial that freely reifies archetypal entities, after the manner
of Vajrayana Buddhism. Here is a portion of the memorial *ekomon* used by the
Rochester Zen Center and its legatees:

> Oh Compassionate Ones,
> you who possess the wisdom of understanding, love, and compassion,
> the power of divine deeds and protection in incomprehensible measure:
> [Name of deceased] is passing from this world to the next.
> She/He is taking a great leap.
> The light of this world has faded for her/him.
> She/He has entered solitude with her/his karmic forces.
> She/He has gone into a vast Silence.
> She/He is borne away by the Great Ocean.
> Oh Compassionate Ones,
> protect [name], who is defenseless.
> Be to her/him like a mother and a father.[13]

Other Zen centers have memorials that are similar in spirit. Glenn H. Mullin
makes the interesting point that *ekomon* (which he calls "prayers") do not have
a central place in Mahayana practice (the August Title changed by Myohoji
monks would be an exception). Moreover, they are recited "tongue in cheek,"
with the consciousness that the person reciting the *ekomon,* the *ekomon* itself,
and the act of reciting it — all lack self-nature, inherent value, and status,[14] not
to mention soul and afterlife. And, of course, there is no authority up there to
lend a hand.

"Tongue in cheek" is perhaps not quite the appropriate expression. The
appeal to other powers, whether in some *ekomon* or in the Nembutsu, acknowledges the lack of fortitude one feels on facing the heroic path of self-realization,[15]
or on facing the inexorable inevitability of illness, old age, and death. However, by all accounts the Buddha Shakyamuni attained realization on his own

and reached an altogether good-humored accommodation with the facts of life and death. Subsequent literature bristles with succeeding champions of his Way. Pure Land practices and the *ekomon,* which appeal to other powers, are also subsequent developments. They appeal to the psyche that finds a home in Christianity as well, with its promises of hope and eternal life.

Similarly but not identically, the twenty-fifth chapter of the Lotus Sutra, recited daily as a separate sutra in Zen monasteries in Japan, enumerates the powers of Kanzeon (Ch. *Kuan-shih-yin,* Skt. *Avalokiteshvara*) to save petitioners from tribulations and disasters in this world and to fulfill their desires. By calling out *"Namu kanzeon bosatsu"* a victim of torture will be delivered; a prisoner, whether guilty or not guilty of a crime, will be freed; a merchant transporting valuable commodities will be protected from robbers; a woman may choose to have a male or a female child; and so on.[16] This sutra, however, like so many religious devotions, Buddhist and Christian alike, can be seen as a metaphor. The Zen student finds that Kanzeon is not an outside deity.

ZAZEN

ZAZEN, the practice of focused meditation found in the Zen schools, is best judged by its fruits.

> Yun-yen asked Tao-wu, "How does the Bodhisattva Kuan-shih-yin
> [Kanzeon] use all those many hands and eyes?"
> Tao-wu said, "It is like reaching behind your head for your pillow
> in the middle of the night."[17]

Kanzeon is commonly delineated with multiple arms and eyes by way of presenting her many skillful means to comfort and support. For the Zen student, she is not a denizen of another world, but the noble archetype of the pilgrim who has forgotten the self in the peak experience of the practice. By name she is the "One Who Perceives the Sounds of the World." The crow goes *"caw-caw!"* the sparrow goes *"chirp-chirp!"* The stone striking a stalk of bamboo went *"tock!"* for Hsiang-yen.[18] The drum for Wu-men's noon meal went *"boom!"*[19] Kanzeon's great compassionate power does not arise from her vows, but from her realization. She is the one who *really* perceives sounds. Body and mind drop away and there is only *Tock! Boom!* The metaphor expands to displays, tastes, sensations, and thoughts. The sole self disappears and the multicentered self manifests, large, containing multitudes. "Shakyamuni, seeing the morning star, attained realization and exclaimed, 'I and all beings have at this moment attained the Way.' "[20] To paraphrase Dogen Kigen: No trace of such realization remains, and this no-trace is continued endlessly[21] — as old Tao-wu stretches and yawns.

The passage to such attainment, however, is rigorous. It is focused mediation straight through the void of the forgotten self, as "The Ten Oxherding Pictures" show vividly.[22] The Desert Fathers agree ("Apply yourself to silence").[23] This is *shikantaza,* the act of pure sitting, which transcends yet includes the world of the sacred and profane.[24] Hotei (Ch. Pu-tai) can then appear in the city with his bag full of candy for the children, mingling with prostitutes and publicans and saving them all[25] — reminiscent of Desert Fathers, not to mention Sufi and Hasidist masters. *Listen to the Desert:* "A certain old man was asked, 'What is necessary to do in order to be saved?' The old man was making rope and, without looking up, he said, 'You are looking at it.' "[26]

THE VOW

THE VOW is part of this same rigorous passage, and like many other Buddhist practices, tends to be grounded in first-person responsibility. The Four Bodhisattva Vows, traced to Chih-i, founder of the T'ien-t'ai tradition, are based line by line on the Four Noble Truths, and are recited in all Mahayana sanctuaries in slightly different wordings at the close of virtually all ceremonies:

> Beings are countless, I vow to save them all;
> Defilements are inexhaustible, I vow to end them all;
> The teachings are innumerable, I vow to master them all;
> The path to Buddhahood is unsurpassed. I vow to attain it.[27]

Also essential to the Buddha Way are the Refuge Vows, the entry into commitment, rooted in earliest practice:

> I take refuge in the Buddha;
> I take refuge in the Dharma;
> I take refuge in the Sangha.

Though classically the first of the Refuge Vows refers to Gautama,[28] the Mahayana understanding, as explained by my teachers, would be finding my home in his realization. I find my home in the teaching as well, and in the kinship with pilgrims on the path. These Three Vows of Refuge, together with the Three Pure Precepts — to avoid all evil, practice all good, and save the many beings, derived from the *Dhammapada,* [29] and the Ten Grave Precepts (also derived from Classical Buddhism[30]) form the Sixteen Bodhisattva Precepts, the core of *Jukai* and ordination ceremonies in Mahayana schools.[31]

Thus, unlike the *ekomon,* the vow has a central place in the Mahayana. In his study *The Bodhisattva Doctrine in Sanskrit Literature,* Har Dayal traces *bodhichitta,* the aspiration for enlightenment, developing in importance in the Mahayana to enlightenment, developing in importance in the Mahayana to formalization as *pranidhana* and the pronouncement of vows, to incorporation among the Ten Paramitas.[32]

The Sixteen Bodhisattva Vows are ritualized, but informal expressions of determination also have an important place in Buddhist practice. The vows of the Buddha Shakyamuni not to leave his place under the Bodhi tree until he had achieved his purpose of realization are renewed in Zen monasteries by each novice, and are the central imperative of most Mahayana schools.[33] Similar expressions of determination are also found in the life stories of Christians, humble and famous. Brother Lawrence, for example, determined that he would practice the presence of God for the rest of his days, whether or not his anxieties were pacified.[34]

The vows presented in the Pure Conduct Chapter of the *Hua-yen ching* (J. *Kegon Kyo, Flower Ornament Sutra*) are not ritualized but are specific to everyday situations. The Bodhisattva Manjushri is asked an elaborate, lengthy question about how Bodhisattvas can attain wisdom and compassion. He replies with 139 vows in *gatha* form that set forth occasions to follow the Buddha Way.[35] The first line of the *gatha* establishes the occasion, the second line presents the act of vowing, and the last two lines follow through with the specific conduct that one promises to undertake in the circumstances.

> Washing the dirt from my body
> I vow with all beings
> be pure, regulated and compliant
> and ultimately without defilement.[36]

These *gatha* present actions that are potent with teaching. Often phenomena have the same vigorous function:

> When I see a pond or a lake
> I vow with all beings
> to perfect the karma of speech
> and become skillful at preaching the Dharma.[37]

Skillful speech flows naturally from a serene mind. The pond and the act of bathing are among the myriad things that can advance and confirm the self in peak experience, and similarly they are teachers of religious practice. The ten thousand Tathagata come forth, sacred, as they are, to keep us on the path. I am reminded of the Desert Father Saint Anthony: "A certain philosopher asked St. Anthony: 'Father, how can you be so happy when you are deprived of the consolation of books?' Anthony replied, 'My book, O philosopher, is the nature of created things, and any time I want to read the words of God, the book is before me.'"[38]

God the creator brings forth the ten thousand things to instruct us, but for the Zen Buddhist, at any rate, the created and the creator are one and the same. "The mind is the mountains, the rivers, and the great Earth, the sun, the moon, and the stars," as Dogen Kigen was fond of saying.[39] They teach us, and the fact that they teach us, teaches us.

I have a friendly disagreement with Professor David Chappell, whose translation of the Four Bodhisattva Vows I cite above. He renders the third line, "The teachings are innumerable, I vow to master them all." In the Diamond Sangha, we chant, "Dharma gates are countless, I vow to wake to them." The sweet piping of the linnet! The scent of the *puakinikini!* See the dolphins frolicking around the bow!

> And hark, how blithe the throstle sings;
> He, too, is no mean preacher;
> Come forth into the light of things,
> Let nature be your teacher.[40]

I do see Dr. Chappell's point, however. I trust that he sees mine.

The role of the many beings to nurture and confirm the self is evinced also on *takuhatsu* (Ch. *t'o-po,* Skt. *pindipata*), the walk of monks through the town to accept *dana* of rice or money. Zen monks call out *"Ho!"* as they walk, but this, as head monks of Ryutaku Monastery explained to me, is not the *"ho"* of the Sino-Japanese for "dharma," but rather the first segment of *hoben,* "appropriate means" (Ch. *feng-pien,* Skt. *upaya*), in this case the ripening of chances to circulate the gift. *"Ho!"* is the reminder to townspeople that they too may turn the dharma wheel, and thus enable it to be turned further, and on around.

SANGE

THE DHARMA WHEEL can also be turned with *sange,* or confession, a practice to be distinguished at the outset from Christian, particularly Roman Catholic, confession.[41] There is no original sin to be forgiven by God, but rather a shared realization of the essential purity of *shunyata* as the nature of all things. With this realization in peak experience, all the evil of the past is purified. This is *mushosen* (Ch. *wu-sheng-chang*), repentance on realizing the unborn — that all is pure from the beginning.[42]

Buddhist literature does not give transgressors a circumscribed place after they are redeemed, as the moon was assigned by Dante in his *Paradiso* to priests and nuns who have broken their vows and forgiven. Rather, the Buddha Way is full redemption in the realization of the vacancy of karma and the purity of essential nature, and then renewed realization with renewed confession.[43]

Here is the *sange gatha* that is part of every Rinzai and Soto Zen Buddhist sutra service, as recited in Diamond Sangha centers:

> All the evil karma, ever created by me since of old, on account
> of my beginningless greed, hatred, and ignorance,
> born of my conduct, speech, and thought,
> I now confess openly and fully.[44]

Dogen Kigen says, "If you repent in this way, you will surely have the assistance of the invisible Buddhas and ancestors."[45] Hee-Jin Kim comments, "These acts of repentance and confession are performed in the nondual context of the I who confesses and the Buddhas who receive the confession. . . . Ultimately one confesses, repents, and is forgiven in the non-dual purity of the self and Buddha."[46]

The *sange* ceremony — in the simple form of repeating the *gatha* at daily sutra services, and in more elaborate form of repeating the *gatha* at daily sutra services, and in even more elaborate forms in full-moon ceremonies — is a reminder that the peak experience of realization and redemption must be sustained. Moreover, the process does not stop there. Public confession and repentance are classically a part of conflict resolution in the Buddhist community. See, for example, Thich Nhat Hanh's *Old Path White Clouds,* for the ceremony called *Saptadhikarana-samantha,* the Seven Practices of Reconciliation.[47]

MUDRA AND DHARANI

MUDRA AND *DHARANI* are presentations fundamental to esoteric Buddhism — Shingon in Japan, and the Vajrayana of Tibet and Mongolia. Both are present in exoteric paths of Buddhism as well, though they usually function in supportive roles.

A *mudra* is a "seal," authenticating and personalizing an aspect of realization and its dharma. E. Dale Saunders, in his seminal study *Mudra,* traces its beginnings back to the dramatic gestures of earliest dance. Hindu and then Buddhist iconography reflect its adoption in the hand positions and postures found in archetypal sculpture. In Shingon Buddhism, and in its antecedents in Vajrayana, the *mudra* itself is the practice, with directories listing as many as 295 positions, in two main categories, those presenting aspects of the *kongokai* (Ch. *chin-kang-chiai,* Skt. *Vajradhatu*), the diamond realm of enlightenment, and *taizokai* (Ch. *t'ai-ts-ang-chai,* Skt. *garbhadhatu*), the womb or matrix realm of fundamental wisdom, from which the *kongokai* arises.[48]

The *Gassho-in* (Ch. *ho-chang-yin,* Skt. *anjali mudra*), hands held up palm to palm, is a universal Buddhist gesture of accord, veneration, and respect, and is found across the spectrum of world religions. In Christianity, the sign of the cross could be considered a *mudra,* as well as the ritualized gestures of the priest during mass. The hand position in *zazen,* the *join* (Ch. *ting-yin,* Skt. *dhyana mudra*), with the right hand over the left (sometimes reversed) and the thumbs touching, forms the "mystic triangle" that is found in earliest Indian Buddhist sculpture.

Postures, or *asana* (J. *za*, Ch. *tso*), are bodily *mudra*, so to speak. The figure of the Buddha in meditation might first come to mind. With hands in *join*, the Zen student presents the Buddha himself or herself beneath the Bodhi tree. There are a large number of other postures in Zen and other Buddhist traditions, with leg and hand positions defining the variations.[49]

Saunders does not include bows among *mudra*, but surely the standing bow and the prostration fit the category. *Raihai* (Ch. *li-pai*, Skt. *namas-kara*), the bow to the floor, is found throughout Buddhism, in Christian ordination, and in other world religions, with variations in leg positions and hand placement. Christian genuflection is a kind of abbreviated prostration. The Zen student is taught that in *raihai* one throws everything away. Pivoting the forearms on the elbows and raising the hands while prostrated is the act of raising the Buddha's feet above one's head.

The *dharani* is the verbal seal of a rite, again found as a central practice in Shingon and Vajrayana, but also a seal of a sutra or a series of sutras in Zen and other Mahayana traditions. The briefer mantra, not distinguished from the *dharani* in Far Eastern etymology, can also be a seal, or it may stand alone as a sacred formula. The Nembutsu, the *Daimoku*, the supplication to Kanzeon, and the call of monks on *takuhatsu* can be considered mantra.

Like other *dharani* and some mantra, the closing words of the *Heart Sutra* are mostly bastard Sanskrit that nobody translates satisfactorily, in this case a kind of "Ode to Joy." Here is the Sino-Japanese, spaced to the beat of the sutra:

> *Gya te gya te, pa ra gya te, para so gya te*
> *bo ji sowa ka, han nya shin gyo.*[50]

It is interesting that the *Heart Sutra* refers to itself as a *dharani* or mantra, recalling the identity of wisdom and words emphasized by Dogen Kigen and Meister Eckhart alike.[51]

The Zen sutra service in the West has inherited *dharani* from Japan, including the *"Shosai Myo Kichijo Darani,"* a short ode to Kichijo-ten (Skt. *Lakshmi*), incarnation of good fortune and merit. This is traditionally recited three times following the *Heart Sutra* "to remove disasters." Another, the *"Daihi Shin Darani,"* dedicated to Kanzeon, the incarnation of mercy, is longer and is recited seven times. Like the "ode to joy" at the end of the *Heart Sutra,* these *dharani* are rationally almost meaningless incantations, and D. T. Suzuki's efforts to translate them, he admits, are problematic.[52] Nonetheless, they are meaningful to those who gather to recite them, simply, it seems, by the chanting itself. I feel that Gregorian chants, though straightforward in meaning, have something of *dharani* quality, and perhaps this was sensed by my teacher Nakagawa Soen Roshi, who spent many hours listening to them on recordings, though he had no understanding of the language.

The short *Enmei Jikku Kannon Gyo (Ten-Verse Kannon Sutra of Timeless Life)*, though readily translatable, also has a *dharani*-like quality.[53] In early Diamond Sangha days I offered a translation for recitation in lieu of the Sino-Japanese original, and it was shouted down after a trial of only a few days. There was just too much en*chant*ment (sorry!) in the old rhythms.

SUTRAS AND SUTRA SERVICES

SUTRA SERVICES in Buddhism, like Christian singing, can be deeply moving experiences. In the Gelugpa sect of Tibetan Buddhism, sutras are chanted in a profound monotone that requires special training, a practice that carries over into other esoteric Mahayana sects. Sutras in the exoteric sects in Japan are recited in a less profound monotone, and in all other Buddhist cultures they are rendered in a kind of plain song, with Korean and Burmese chants especially beautiful. Again the comparison to Gregorian chanting comes to mind — and Moslem chanting, Judaic chanting, Hindu chanting, traditional peoples' chanting across the world. Surely there is no religious practice more universal than vocalizing.

Perhaps even more closely than Gregorian chants, the Buddhist sutra services are linked to the very founder of the religion, for they evoke the recitations of the Buddha's sermons of earliest times. Ananda, it is said, had perfect recall, and all sutras begin with his words "Thus have I heard," which prefaced his training of teachers at the first assembly of elders after the Buddha's death. For the next five hundred years, all sutras were transmitted orally.[54] Even today, the constant oral repetition of words — for example in the *Heart Sutra:* "Form is emptiness; / emptiness is form" — in the context of related expressions of the teaching establishes a frame for realization of the Buddha's views. Ananda K. Coomaraswamy makes a strong case for illiteracy in the setting of a strong oral tradition, for the old words are deeply imprinted, like the poetry a grandmother reads to her little grandchildren. They are not merely words one reads on a printed page.[55]

This internalizing enhances the religious course. Saint Augustine of Hippo said, "He who sings prays twice."[56] I would suggest also that those who chant as incantation "pray" more than once as well, and when the incantation aspect of singing or chanting is removed, many of the most religious feel deprived, as Catholic congregations felt to one degree or another when their services were converted from Latin — as my own students felt when the *Enmei Jikku Kannon Gyo* was translated. Moreover, the profound benefits of singing and chanting play themselves out in physical health and well-being, and indeed as research anecdotal evidence indicates, chanting, singing, and reciting aloud (and hearing this vocalizing) lie at the very well-springs of human integration and inspiration.[57]

CONCLUSION

I AM SURE there are other practices that are analogous in Buddhism and Christianity, but for our purposes, these seven seem to suffice. What, then, is my comparison?

Most importantly, the presence of God sets the tone for Christian prayer, from the formulas of children and the assurances of Brother Lawrence to the plain but profound utterances of the Desert Fathers and the "blasphemy" of Meister Eckhart: "We pray God to rid us of 'God' so that we may grasp and enjoy the truth, where the highest angel and the fly and the soul are equal."[58] God must guide us to the elimination of his concept, that all things might be seen in their equality. For Yuan-wu, however, the commentator on *The Blue Cliff Record,* it is with individual human realization that the many beings are seen in their glorious light, and the Buddhas, sages, and masters, not to mention God or "God," have no role whatever, and are, in fact, excluded: "If you turn upwards, then even Shakyamuni, Manjushri, Samantabhadra, and the myriad sages, together with all the masters in the world, all suck in their breaths and swallow their voices. If you turn downwards, worms and maggots and everything that crawls, all sentient beings, each and every one emits great shining light."[59]

Thus, there is a huge difference. Teachers smile out at the audience at the conference of comparative religion. They have two nostrils each, two ears, one chin apiece, but their robes and their practices disclose their diversity. "Yes, but..." marks their discourse.

Chacun à son goût.

NOTES

1. D. T. Suzuki, *A Miscellany on the Shin Teaching of Buddhism* (Kyoto: Shinshu Otaniha Shumusho, 1949), 71–91.

2. "Instructions Given by Mrs. Mori to Her Son," ibid., 72–73.

3. Thomas Merton, *The Wisdom of the Desert: Sayings from the Desert Fathers of the Fourth Century* (New York: New Directions, 1960), 20.

4. William Doheny, *Selected Writings of St. Teresa of Avila* (Milwaukee: Bruce Publishing Co., 1950), 20.

5. Shantideva, *The Bodhicaryavatara,* trans. Kate Crosby and Andrew Skilton (New York: Oxford University Press, 1998), 138.

6. Robert Aitken, *Encouraging Words: Zen Buddhist Teachings for Western Students* (San Francisco: Pantheon, 1993), 195–96.

7. See Nichidatsu Fujii, *Buddhism, for World Peace* (n.p.: Japan-Bharat Sarvodaya Mitrata Sangha, 1980) and Jacqueline Stone, "Chanting the August Title of the *Lotus Sutra:* Daimoku Practices in Classical and Medieval Japan," in *Revisioning Kamakura Buddhism,* ed. Richard K. Payne (Honolulu: University of Hawai'i Press, 1998).

8. Sharon Salsberg, *Loving Kindness: The Revolutionary Art of Happiness* (Boston: Shambhala, 1995), 32.

9. Ibid., 18.

10. John Blofeld, *The Zen Teaching of Huang Po* (New York: Grove, 1958), 30.

11. Mev Puleo, *The Struggle Is One: Voices and Visions of Liberation* (Albany: State University of New York Press, 1994), 14, 22, 25, 29.

12. Matthew Fox, *Breakthrough: Meister Eckhart's Creation Spirituality in New Translation* (New York: Doubleday, 1980), 66.

13. Message from David Dunley, Office Manager, Denver Zen Center, July 5, 2000.

14. Glenn H. Mullin,"Prayer," *Tricycle: The Buddhist Magazine* 9, no. 3 (Spring 2000): 77.

15. D. T. Suzuki, "The Development of the Pure Land Doctrine," *Collected Writings on Shin Buddhism,* ed. the Eastern Buddhist Society (Kyoto: Shinshu Otaniha, 1973), 11.

16. Burton Watson, *The Lotus Sutra* (New York: Columbia University Press, 1993), 299–300.

17. Cf. Thomas and J. C. Cleary, *The Blue Cliff Record* (Boston: Shambhala, 1992), 489.

18. Robert Aitken, *The Gateless Barrier: The Wu-men kuan (Mumonkan)* (San Francisco: North Point, 1990), 39.

19. Ibid., 4.

20. Cf. Thomas Cleary, *Transmission of Light (Denkoroku): Zen in the Art of Enlightenment, by Zen Master Keizan* (San Francisco: North Point, 1990), 3.

21. Dogen Kigen, *Shobogenzo: Genjokoan.* Cf. Hee-Jin Kim, *Flowers of Emptiness: Selections from Dogen's Shobogenzo* (Lewiston, N.Y.: Edwin Mellon, 1985), 52.

22. D. T. Suzuki, *Manual of Zen Buddhism* (Kyoto: Eastern Buddhist Society, 1935), 150–61; plates II–XI.

23. Merton, *The Wisdom of the Desert,* 47.

24. Carl Bielefeldt, *Dogen's Manuals of Meditation* (Berkeley: University of California Press, 1988), 184.

25. Suzuki, *Manual of Zen Buddhism,* 161; plate XI.

26. Gregory Mayers, *Listen to the Desert: Secrets of Spiritual Maturity from the Desert Fathers and Mothers* (Liguori, Mo.: Liguori/Triumph, 1996), 105.

27. David Chappell, *T'ien-t'ai Buddhism: An Outline of the Fourfold Teachings* (Tokyo: Daiichi Shobo, 1983), 103.

28. Tevijja Sutta. Maurice Walshe, *Thus Have I Heard: The Long Discourses of the Buddha* (London: Wisdom Publications, 1987), 195.

29. Irving Babbitt, trans., *The Dhammapada* (New York: New Directions, 1965), 30.

30. Har Dayal, *The Bodhisattva Doctrine in Sanskrit Literature* (Delhi: Mitilal Banarsidas, 1934), 193–209.

31. Aitken, *Encouraging Words,* 189–96.

32. Dayal, *The Bodhisattva Doctrine,* 67. See also Robert Aitken, *The Practice of Perfection: The Paramitas from a Zen Buddhist Perspective* (Washington, D.C.: Counterpoint, 1997), 147–84.

33. Giei Sato and Eshin Nishimura, *Unsui: A Diary of Zen Monastic Life* (Honolulu: University of Hawai'i Press, 1973), Pl. 8.

34. Brother Lawrence, *The Practice of the Presence of God* (Springdale, Pa.: Whitaker House, 1982), 10–11.

35. Thomas Cleary, *The Flower Ornament Scripture,* 3 vols. (Boulder, Colo.: Shambhala, 1984–1987), 1:313–29. Hsuan-hua, *Flower Ornament Sutra; Pure Conduct Chapter 11,* 167.

36. Cf. Cleary, ibid., 318, and Hsuan-hua, ibid., 144.

37. Cleary, *Flower Ornament Sutra,* I:321; Hsuan-hua, *Flower Ornament Sutra; Pure Conduct Chapter 11,* 167.

38. Merton, *Wisdom of the Desert,* 62.

39. Dogen Kigen, *Shobogenzo: Sokushin Sokubutsu*. Cf. Gudo Nishimura and Chodo Cross, *Master Dogen's Shobogenzo: Book 1* (Woking, Surrey: Windbell, 1994), 53.

40. "The Tables Turned." *William Wordsworth: Selected Poetry*, ed. Mark Van Doren (New York: Modern Library, 1950), 83.

41. See Quentin Donaghue and Linda Shapiro, *Bless Me Father, For I Have Sinned: Catholics Speak Out about Confession* (New York: Donald I. Fine, 1984).

42. Hisao Inagaki, *A Dictionary of Japanese Buddhist Terms: Based on References in Japanese Literature* (Union City, Calif.: Heian International, 1989), 520. Two other types of *sange* are cited in the same entry: (1) ritual confession before an image of the Buddha (J. *sahosen*, Ch. *tso-fa-chang*); and (2) confession in meditation before a visualized Buddha who then strokes the head of the penitent one (J. *shusosen*, Ch. *chu-hsiang-chang*).

43. For early accounts of redemption on realizing the pure vacancy of karma, see the story of the serial murderer Angulimala and his encounter with the Buddha in *The Middle Length Discourses of the Buddha: A New Translation of the Majjhima Nikaya*, trans. Bhikkhu Nanamoli and Bhikkhu Bodhi (Boston: Wisdom Publications, 1995), 710–17; and the account of two monks guilty of sexual violence and murder who found redemption with Vimalakirti, after failing to find it with Upali, in *The Vimalakirti Sutra*, trans. Burton Watson (New York: Columbia University Press, 1997), 46–48.

44. Cf. D. T. Suzuki's translation in his *The Training of the Zen Buddhist Monk* (Kyoto: Eastern Buddhist Society, 1934); 47, also his citation of the formal confessions of Torei, Ta-hui, and Chung-feng, which are recited in Rinzai sutra services. Ibid., 48–50.

45. Dogen Kigen, *Shobogenzo: Keisei Sanahoku*, cited by Hee-Jin Kim, *Dogen Kigen: Mystical Realist* (Tucson: University of Arizona Press, 1987), 205.

46. Ibid., 205–6.

47. Thich Nhat Hanh, *Old Path White Clouds: Walking in the Footsteps of the Buddha* (Berkeley, Calif.: Parallax Press, 1991), 311–13.

48. E. Dale Saunders, *Mudra: A Study of Symbolic Gestures in Japanese Buddhist Sculpture* (Princeton, N.J.: Princeton University Press, 1985), 3, 11–12.

49. Ibid., 121–31.

50. Aitken, *Encouraging Words*, 175.

51. Donald Lopez Jr., *The Heart Sutra Explained: Indian and Tibetan Commentaries* (Albany: State University of New York Press, 1988), 125; Dogen Kigen, *Shobogenzo: Mitsugo*, cited by Hee-Jin Kim, *Dogen Kigen: Mystical Realist* (Tucson: University of Arizona Press, 1987), 78; Eckhart, "A Flowing Out but Returning Within." Fox, *Breakthrough*, 65–69.

52. Suzuki, *Manual of Zen Buddhism*, 12.

53. Aitken, *Encouraging Words*, 178.

54. Kogen Mizuno, *Buddhist Sutras: Origin, Development, Transmission* (Tokyo: Kosei Publishing Co., 1982), 18.

55. Ananda K. Coomaraswamy, "The Bugbear of Literacy," in *Am I My Brother's Keeper?* (New York: John Day, 1947), 19–35.

56. United States Catholic Conference, Inc., *Catechism of the Catholic Church for the United States of America* (Liguori, Mo.: Liguori Publications, 1994), 299.

57. See Alfred A. Tomatis, *The Conscious Ear: My Life of Transformation through Listening* (Barrytown, N.Y.: Station Hill Press, 1991), particularly 198–230.

58. Fox, *Breakthrough*, 215.

59. Cf. Cleary and Cleary, *The Blue Cliff Record*, 66.

Meditation and Prayer:
A Comparative Inquiry

RITA M. GROSS

University of Wisconsin – Eau Claire

A FAMOUS PRAYER that many would associate with the Christian tradition states: "God, grant me the serenity to accept what I cannot change, the courage to change what I can, and the wisdom to know the difference." If I use that prayer, however, I say simply "Grant me the serenity to accept what I cannot change, the courage to change what I can, and the wisdom to know the difference." Despite the fact that many assume that Buddhists do not send forth such verbal requests, I have no hesitation concerning this modified version of the "serenity prayer" because it has so many Buddhist analogues.

In this paper, I will be concerned with three questions. The first is the correctness of the usual impression that prayer is utterly foreign to the nontheistic character of Buddhism. The second question, based upon a negative answer to the first, asks why a nontheistic religion engages in prayer, given that it seems to imply a recipient or listener. Finally, the most theoretical question and hypothetical question concerns what difference, if any, could be posited in the religious experience of praying theists and praying nontheists. One version of the serenity prayer quoted above calls upon "God," while the other omits that reference point. That difference in form does reflect major theological differences between Buddhism and Christianity. However, the more interesting question is whether this linguistic shift makes any difference in the experiences of the people praying or in the results of their prayers. Does this serenity prayer have a different effect on me, a Buddhist, than on a Christian, all other things being equal? While empirical studies to test whether differences occur are probably impossible to devise, I would not be surprised to find that these theological opposites mask similarity of experience and results.

Because Buddhism and Christianity often seem to be such different religions, in-depth comparative theological analyses between these two traditions are fascinating. What can seem like a clear contrast one minute becomes a surprising similarity the next moment. Crossovers abound. It seems that Buddhism denies the existence of self while Christianity does not; but then some Buddhists talk of the "big I" and Christian teachings often talk about the necessity to "lose the self" before one can find it.[1] In any college course introducing the world's religions, one would be taught that Christianity is a theistic religion, positing a deity separate from humanity, and that Buddhism is one of the world's few nontheistic religions, denying the existence (or, more accurately, the *relevance*) of any transcendent, external supreme being who created the world and bestows salvation on followers of that religion. But then we learn of Pure Land Buddhism, in which one is advised to rely solely on the Other Power of Buddha Amida to assure rebirth in the Pure Land. And so it goes.

On the surface, it would appear that a theological continental divide looms in the purported difference between meditation and prayer, a theological divide that should make the phrase "Buddhist prayer" an oxymoron and should make Buddhists unwilling to utter something like the serenity prayer. It is often taught in introductory courses in world religions that, because of the theological difference between a theistic and a nontheistic religion, Christians *pray*, whereas Buddhists *meditate*. Often a stark contrast is posited; prayer is verbal, filled with words, addressing another being, whereas meditation is nonverbal, a silent noting of the breath. But that differentiation tells only part of the story. The nonverbal silent meditation that many associate with Buddhism is only one form of Buddhist meditation; Buddhist practice also includes many verbal utterances. Furthermore, when many Tibetan Buddhists use the English language, they use the word "prayer" quite freely. For example, after the terrorist attacks on New York City and Washington, D.C., in September 2001, the Dalai Lama conducted what he called a "prayer service" for the many victims. Thus, it is not so surprising that a Buddhist could feel quite comfortable uttering the serenity prayer without the initial word "God" and feel that it is an effective and meaningful utterance. Nor is it unknown for Christians at prayer to simply give themselves over to a wordless attempt to conform to God's will. Clearly, something more subtle is occurring than a distinction between Christians engaging in word-filled request prayers to a personal deity and Buddhists wordlessly and impersonally noting the breath. No area of comparative Buddhist-Christian studies is more fascinating than that of prayer and meditation. Nor are crossovers more common in any other area of comparative Buddhist-Christian studies.

Even more surprising, many Buddhist religious utterances *do* seem to invoke some presence, some "other" whom one is addressing. For example, consider the following religious utterance:

> Hold me with the treasury of your love.
> You who are the refuge,
> Protect me from the terrifying sufferings of existence, such as
> Birth, old age, sickness, death and so on,
> And completely liberate all my defilements.[2]

If one were simply presented with this prayer and asked to identify its source, say on an exam in an introductory religious studies course, the average student could be forgiven for assuming that this utterance is definitely not Buddhist and might perhaps be from the Christian tradition. Even someone reasonably well acquainted with religious traditions might surmise that this is a Christian prayer, given the clear language of address, implicating a being separate from oneself, and the petitionary character of the statement. Someone well acquainted with the conventions of Buddhist religious expressions might find a clue in the stock phrase "sufferings of existence, such as birth, old age, sickness, death and so on." These were identified by the Buddha in his first sermon as the first four of the eight types of suffering detailed in the First Noble Truth and are quite common in Buddhist liturgies. Perhaps even more mystifying than a Buddhist prayer that seems to posit a being to whom one could pray is that the fact that the being who has just been petitioned for very concrete and basic benefits dissolves "through non-conceptualization into the state of radiant emptiness" a few lines later in the liturgy.[3] What is the point of such seemingly "theistic" language if the deity being invoked does not really exist as such, independently and eternally?

This utterance is indeed from a Buddhist liturgy, and not from a popular tradition in which various "super-human" beings are routinely invoked. This statement is from an esoteric and advanced form of Vajrayana Buddhism, which is adamantly nontheistic and nondualistic in its metaphysics. Such statements lead me to suggest that if one did not know on some other basis that Buddhism is a nontheistic tradition, one could never figure that out from reading Buddhist liturgies, even liturgies that deal with advanced meditation practices. On the contrary, at least in the Tibetan Vajrayana tradition, such liturgies are filled with confessions, offerings, praises, and requests for blessings and many other boons. Thus, the form found in such Buddhist liturgies is at least superficially similar to many familiar Christian forms of address to the deity, despite the theological differences. Why? What is going on? And are the inner psychological experiences of the prayer and the meditator relatively similar, given the similarity of the verbal forms, or relatively different because of the theological differences?

At least three different types of Buddhist verbal utterances, or "prayers," can be distinguished, and the theology and religious experience connected with these three different forms can provide some clues to discussing the question of just how similar or different prayer and meditation actually are. The first type of Buddhist prayer, somewhat unknown to many outsiders, involves prayer to many relatively existing beings. The second type of prayer involves making aspirations or wishes, in which no one is addressed, but many hopes are expressed. The third, most elusive type of Buddhist utterance comes from the liturgies of Tibetan "deity yoga," such as the one quoted above. Forms of address in a nondualistic, nontheistic theological context could seem like a theological absurdity. There must be some explanation at the level of religious psychology that justifies using such forms as a "skillful means" to promote spiritual transformation, with the result that these nontheistic *forms* are very similar to their theistic cousins.

The first level of exploration should center on some of the beings to whom Buddhists routinely "pray" and on their existential status. In this case, both the religious forms and the theology, I would argue, are reasonably similar in Buddhism and Christianity. Prayers are addressed to beings experienced as separate from oneself, from whom one asks for various boons and benefits. Even the forms of Buddhism that are most rigorous and uncompromising about ultimate nontheism have always recognized that super-human beings, invisible to ordinary human vision, do indeed "exist" and can be petitioned, just as believers in deities petition their deities, who are also invisible. Buddhists also believe that petitions to such beings can be effective, can change the course of events, just as theists believe that their prayers have an effect. Furthermore, Buddhists have *always* believed in the existence of such beings. These beliefs and practices are not due to a later degeneration from a pure early form of Buddhism. Otherwise early Buddhists could not have told stories about the historical Buddha being urged to preach his dharma by various divine beings who told him that his preaching would be effective, despite his initial doubts that anyone would understand his teachings.

Only modern North American converts to Buddhism have trouble recognizing the existence of these beings and relating with them, precisely because of the way in which they understand nontheism. North American Buddhists tend to assume that beings whom they cannot access with their senses, beings who apparently have no empirical existence, do not exist in any way and that this is the meaning of "nontheism." But classically, Buddhist nontheism is not about the *relative* nonexistence of such beings, but about their *absolute* nonexistence. At the level of relative truth, such beings exist and there is no more reason why a Buddhist should not pray, confess wrongdoings, or engage in praise, thanksgiving, and offering liturgies to them than why a Christian would not do the same. And they might pray for many of the same things: reversal of negative fortunes, health, wealth, and well-being in general. That for which a Buddhist cannot pray, but a Christian might, is more ultimate — enlightenment or salvation. There is no possibility of vicarious enlightenment in Buddhism and no deity can confer it, because enlightenment is a matter of clearing away confusion and uncovering one's primordial pure and enlightened state. However, my impression is that Christians also believe that human *acceptance* of salvation is necessary, that God does not "save" human beings indiscriminately or randomly. And even Buddhists pray that the *obstacles* to enlightenment might be lessened or destroyed.

What does it mean to say that the beings to whom Buddhists pray "exist"? The understanding of "existence" is quite different from that which a Christian would affirm about God. But it is not so different from what a Christian might affirm about the existence of saints or angels. According to Buddhism, deities exist in the same way that we humans exist. To ourselves we feel very real, but analysis clearly demonstrates that there is no substantial, lasting, permanent self. In the same way, deities can be encountered, but analysis finds no grounds for positing a truly external, independently existing deity. Instead, everything consists of a matrix of interdependence and is, therefore, empty of inherent existence. But that does not mean that things are altogether, utterly nonexistent. In fact, such nihilistic interpretations of emptiness are considered to be extremely dangerous spiritually. For us, what is important is that such beings exist independently of us ordinary, unenlightened human beings. We do not think them up any more than we conjure up our own relative existence. So long as it seems to us that we exist, they also exist and they can be of help or hindrance to us. For a person who still believes in his or her own ego, his or her own existence, as do all unenlightened beings, to declare that saints, angels, and inhabitants of traditional Buddhist universes do not exist is merely a matter of confused understanding.

However, in a Buddhist framework, such beings do not exist independently of the insight of an enlightened being, who can see them for what they are — ultimately nonexistent as independent beings. Thus they are denied the total independence that Christians posit of God. It would seem, at least vis-à-vis human beings, that saints and angels exist in the same way. They do not exist independent of God, but they do exist independent of human beings, just as do the myriad nonhuman, nonempirical beings who populate any traditional Buddhist universe. Only when we truly understand our own emptiness, our own lack of inherent existence will we truly see that deities do not inherently exist either. Until then, we might as well pray to them, and Buddhists do. There seems no reason to assume that the inner experience of a Buddhist petitioning for general well-being or for help on the spiritual path is significantly different from that a Christian praying to God or the saints for similar things.

Buddhist prayers to such relatively existing beings are only the most mundane form of Buddhist prayer. Buddhists also routinely make utterances in which they wish for many positive things: the well-being of all sentient beings; the fulfillment of the vision of a great teacher; or our own ability to gain wisdom and compassion, so that we could be truly helpful. This kind of utterance is often called an "aspiration" because it expresses ideals or goals toward which we are striving. In Buddhist terms, the serenity prayer, minus the single word "God," would be an aspiration prayer, which helps explain why it is so unproblematic to Buddhists. A famous Buddhist aspiration prayer comes from early Buddhism and is widespread in the contemporary Buddhist world. Often called the Four

Immeasurables or the Four Divine Abodes (a literal translation of the Pali), the request is as follows:

> May all sentient beings enjoy happiness and the root of happiness,
> May they be free from suffering and the root of suffering.
> May they not be separated from the great happiness devoid of suffering.
> May they dwell in the great equanimity free from passion, aggression, and
>   bewilderment.[4]

These four are also known simply as friendliness, compassion, sympathetic joy, and equanimity, considered to be the enlightened or useful emotions. Other common aspirations express the wish for one's own progress on the path and eventual enlightenment. For example:

> Through all my births may I not be separated from the perfect guru
> And so enjoy the splendor of dharma.
> Perfecting the virtues of the paths and stages,
> May I speedily attain the state of Vajradhara [ultimate enlightenment].[5]

Another variant of this theme is the "dedication of merit." Again this practice is widespread in Buddhism and is found in the forms of Buddhism least given to dealings with any kind of super-human, nonempirical beings. Considered to be an essential expression of egolessness or the lack of a permanent substantial self, in this verbal utterance, one gives away any merit that may have accrued due to spiritual practice or virtuous activity, transferring it from oneself to all sentient beings.

> By this merit may all obtain omniscience
> May it defeat the enemy, wrongdoing.
> From the stormy waves of birth, old age, sickness and death,
> From the ocean of samsara may I free all beings.[6]

But what is going on in these aspirations? These aspirations are not addressed to the relatively existing beings who receive more mundane requests. In fact, there is no "you" to whom they are addressed, only an "I" making the aspiration and recipients of the wishes expressed in the aspiration or dedication. Buddhists do not believe that there is an all-powerful being who could make these things happen independent of human striving (and probably Christians also don't believe that these things will happen without human cooperation with the divine). So what is the point? Why bother, if there is no one to whom these requests could be addressed? I have, in fact, encountered religious nontheists from a monotheistic background (Unitarian-Universalists to be more specific) who were uncomfortable with these simple Buddhist aspirations. They were equally uncomfortable with the serenity prayer. Their discomfort stemmed from the fact that, as they saw things, these statements could not be "true," because there is no being who could hear or react to a dedication of merit, the Four Immeasurables, or the serenity prayer.

At this point, we may simply encounter a basic difference in psychological styles, which is why it is fortunate that there are so many religious paths. Some people simply cannot abide any form of ritual or anything that is not completely rational and empirical. To them, practices like Buddhist aspiration prayers seem "superstitious," because they could not possibly really magically transform the world's suffering and confusion. They would probably say that such transformation requires hard work in the world, not prayer, or even mindfulness meditations that focus solely on the breath and the body. These are luxuries that a troubled world can ill afford, they might claim.

Others, however, would point to the effect that utterances such as the Four Immeasurables can have on the one who *says or thinks them*. Whatever else may or may not happen in prayer and religious ritual, well-crafted prayers and liturgies have a clear, demonstrable impact on those who participate in them. Such prayers are about and for the religious *subject*, the person who regularly remembers aspirations such as the Four Immeasurables and fervently, longingly imagines that he or she is able to live out these aspirations fully. Contemplating the Four Immeasurables helps one become a person who can actually manifest them. Phenomonologically, such utterances *are not* primarily for or about a purported listener, the nonexistent or unresponsive God who doesn't snap his or her fingers and make the aspirations come true, whatever theology may claim.

If this is the case, prayer works, whether or not any external being hears or responds to prayers. Buddhists have always known this, which explains why even Buddhists who believe that the Buddha has passed entirely beyond this realm and does not hear or respond to petitions venerate, bow, and make offerings to him. Such Buddhists know and believe that these behaviors will have a positive effect on their state of mind and their behavior. In a monotheistic culture in which people are more concerned with the existence of God than with the psychological effects of religious practice, such explanations for the effectiveness of prayer are often overlooked and such justifications for religious practices might be denigrated. But for Buddhists, with our intense concern with *method*, with what works to develop and transform people spiritually, the impact of a practice on the religious subject is of utmost importance. Buddhists use aspiration prayers because we are more likely to come closer to the ideals expressed in the aspiration with the prayer than without it. Thought is very powerful in the Buddhist system of things. It is better to wish that all beings were happy than to wish difficulties upon them.

However, such reflections on the reasons to pray are not altogether foreign to a theistic context. Sometimes theists reflect that it really couldn't make that much difference to the Lord of the Universe what people do on Saturday or Sunday, whether they eat pork and shellfish, or whether they pray regularly, correctly, and at the proper times. Such practices are done, it is explained, not because God needs these prayers, but because people need them. People need them to form identity and community, to develop discipline, and to feel connected with the source of life. Theists also will explain that people pray because it is helpful to them. Many theists consider prayer to be a form of spiritual cultivation that transforms the one who prays. That function of prayer is certainly an important dimension of the experience of praying. Furthermore, any thoughtful theist should be repulsed by the portrait of God as a vindictive tyrant who gets so mad at people who do not pray properly, enough, or at the proper time, that it unleashes suffering upon such people as punishment. Even in a theistic context, one would have to argue that prayer primarily benefits the religious subject: People need to pray, but God does not need to receive prayers. Thus, theistic prayer and nontheistic meditation again turn out to be more similar than superficial first impressions might indicate. I would strongly argue that though a theological continental divide looms between the theistic and the nontheistic version of the serenity prayer, the experience of the one who utters the prayer and its effect upon that person are more similar than different.

Much more mystifying in the nontheistic context of Buddhism than prayers to relatively existing beings who can help or hinder us, or expressions of the aspirations of Buddhist meditators, are expressions such as the one quoted earlier:

Hold me with the treasury of your love.
You who are the refuge,
Protect me from the terrifying sufferings of existence, such as
Birth, old age, sickness, death and so on,
And completely liberate all my defilements.[7]

These words are addressed to a visualized being whose symbolic form represents ultimate reality and one's own true being. As already mentioned, that being dissolves into light and space later in the liturgy, so whatever existence is attributed to this being, it is not a conventionally existing, solid being. Even more mysterious to outsiders, the visualization practice involves visualizing oneself as this being. So one is not even addressing a being separate from oneself when one says, "Hold me with the treasury of your love." In fact, in an odd way, one is addressing oneself in these practices — one's true being, not one's private ego, of course. Even in liturgies in which one does not identity oneself with the being who is being visualized, eventually that being dissolves into light, which then dissolves into oneself, usually into one's heart center, again emphasizing ultimate theological nonduality.

The metaphysics or theology behind these practices is too complicated to describe fully in this context. In a nutshell, two points are important. First, everything that could possibly be called upon to indicate that there is no duality of self and ultimate reality is utilized in these liturgies. Second, even more important, the splendid beings visualized in these liturgies represent what we really are beneath our cramped, tiny sense of selfhood imprisoned behind our skin and felt to be desperately separate from the rest of reality. The question of the existential status of such beings cannot be answered by appeal to any conventional category. Like everything else, including ourselves who are not different from these beings, ultimately they are beyond the "four extremes,"[8] which is what is meant when the liturgy says that they dissolve "through non-conceptualization into the state of radiant emptiness."[9] Thus, they do not exist in the same way that the deity of Christianity is said to exist, though the assumption that therefore they do not exist is also erroneous. I do not believe that there is a Western equivalent to this "status."

In this context, I am more interested in the praxis, in the intimate, passionate, seemingly dualistic language of address utilized in these visualizations.

Why would such prayerful language be employed in such an utterly nontheistic context? These visualization practices and their attendant verbal liturgies are a "skillful method," something designed to propel the practitioner into recognition of reality as quickly as possible. Thus, such practices are in accord with the fundamental Buddhist assumption that our most basic problem and the root of all suffering is ignorance of what really is the case. We tend to take things, including ourselves, for granted and see them as mundane, meaningless, and not sacred. These liturgies and visualizations stir in us the confidence that such is not the case. They serve as a call, over and over, to awaken to the splendid sacredness of the world and ourselves. A traditional analogy may explain the process: A tiger cub has been raised as a lamb; it bleats and eats grass, not knowing that it is a tiger. One day, it tastes blood and recognizes that it is a tiger, not a sheep. The visualizations and the liturgies are the blood, but apparently a single taste is not enough to transform our identity from duality to nonduality. The skillful means is to taste over and over until we get the flavor of things as they are.

Though the dualistic language of address might seem to be "incorrect" or "not true to reality," the more important concern is whether or not it is effective. Because "truth" is beyond words in any case, Buddhism is willing to use whatever works best to transform the practitioner. There is no question that several facets of our relative existence have great power to move us and to transform us. One is the fact that duality seems real to us, even though we know better, having many times done the analyses that convince us of the error of our conventional belief in duality. By themselves, these analyses do not seem to be able to fully correct our mistaken views. Another facet of our relative existence that is called into service in this type of "prayer" is the effectiveness of words, especially poetic, passionate, intimate words of address. Such language simply appeals to a different level of our being than rational, analytic language, and is much more effective in directing our powerful emotional energies toward awakening. Putting all these together — the seeming reality of duality; the power of symbolic, poetic, passionate and intimate language; and the effectiveness of emotions for transforming consciousness — results in the skillful means of "prayers" such as the one already quoted several times. The only justification and explanation of such practices is that they work. As Chagdud Tulku, Rinpoche, has explained, "Praying to the deity is not a matter of supplicating something outside ourselves.

The point of using a dualistic method, visualizing the deity outside of us, is to overcome duality."[10] He goes on to explain further:

> If the nature of the deity is emptiness, you might wonder why we pray at all. There seems to be a contradiction here. How can we say, on the one hand, that there isn't a deity, only a reflection of our own intrinsic nature, and on the other, that we should pray to it? This makes sense only if we understand the inseparability of absolute and relative truth.
>
> On the absolute level, our nature is buddha, we are the deity. But unaware of this, we're bound by relative truth. In order to make the leap to the realization of our absolute nature, we have to walk on our relative feet, on a relative path. Because absolute truth is so elusive to our ordinary, linear mind, we rely on an increasingly subtle step-by-step process to work with the mind's duality until we achieve recognition. Prayer is an essential part of that process.[11]

Thus, even the case in which the theological differences between Buddhism and Christianity are striking and uncompromising, the forms are more similar than different. What about the experience of a Buddhist doing such a visualization liturgy and a Christian praying? Empirical resolutions of this question are probably impossible to obtain. I *know* when I do this kind of liturgy that I am not praying to an external savior, just as I would imagine most Christians *know* that someone "out there" hears their prayers. However, if that intellectual, verbal part of our multitasking psyche turns off, as sometimes happens, does it *feel* any different?

One might wonder what keeps the Buddhist practitioner from taking these prayers and practices literally and becoming an egomaniac, in which case their effect would be opposite to what is intended. There are two major safeguards. First, the play between form and emptiness is always stressed in these liturgies, so that it would be very difficult for anyone to imagine that the liturgy is about their enduring, solid, permanent identification with a truly existing deity. That misidentification does not seem to occur. More important, these are esoteric practices, limited to those who have been properly prepared, both in terms of philosophical studies and previous meditation practices. These preparations are critical, for giving people access to spiritual practices that they are not prepared to understand and practice correctly does them no favors. Religious esotericism is criticized in many quarters, but in this case at least, there is no alternative. The psychological and spiritual energies being tapped into are too subtle and too powerful for it to be any other way.

NOTES

1. For an example of the "big I," see the famous manual of Zen Buddhism, *Zen Mind: Beginner's Mind.* Suzuki, Shunryu, *Zen Mind: Beginner's Mind; Informal Talks on Zen Meditation Practice* (New York: Weatherhill, 1974), 65–71.

2. From an unpublished Buddhist liturgical text of the Tibetan Nyingma Vajrayana tradition. This quotation is only a single example of a type of religious utterance of which there are countless examples in Tibetan Buddhist liturgies, both esoteric and exoteric.

3. Ibid.

4. A form of this aspiration widely used by Shambhala Buddhist centers.

5. This aspiration is the final verse of a lineage supplication widely used by Tibetan Kagyu Buddhists.

6. One of the dedications of merit widely practiced by the students of Vidydhara, the Venerable Chogyam Trungpa, Rinpoche.

7. See n. 2.

8. Existence, nonexistence, both existence and nonexistence, and neither existence nor nonexistence.

9. See n. 3.

10. Chagdud Tulku, Rinpoche, "Prayer," *Tricycle* 9, no. 3 (Spring 2000): 69.

11. Ibid.

Christian Prayer Seen from the Eye of a Buddhist

KENNETH K. TANAKA

Musashino Women's University, Tokyo

WHEN I THINK about Christian prayer, the image I get is that of a young girl of about eight years old with long brown hair. Wearing a nightgown, she is kneeling next to her bed with her hands clasped and her head bowed. I have often queried myself about the source of this image. This is an interesting question in itself. I personally don't know of anyone who fits that description or who has actually witnessed someone like her in prayer. Nevertheless, it is interesting how a Buddhist raised in a predominately Christian society comes to form his image of Christian prayer.

Working further with this image, I see this little girl — let's call her Megan — doing two things in her evening prayer. One is that she is giving thanks to God for the benefits she has received. She thanks him for her food, clothing, friends, and family. Then, she also makes a request. In this petitionary element of her prayer, she is asking God to make her sick father get well soon. As she does so, her expression turns more serious, and she clasps her hands more firmly and brings them closer to her chest. She then looks up toward the ceiling, expressing her heartfelt wish for her father's early recovery. What is noteworthy is that Megan's prayers are spoken aloud as in a human conversation.

I realize that this image does not do justice to a topic as enormous as "Christian prayer," but I believe that it provides a glimpse into how one Buddhist imagines the topic. I have a number of questions about Megan's prayer, particularly as I try to understand what may be going on inside of her. I wonder first and foremost, what God looks like to her. Is God a male or a female, or neither?

I would think that even for her (in this gender-sensitive age), God is still a male. If so, does she see him as an elderly man with a long white beard, holding a cane and sitting in a throne? Next, where does God reside? If he is in heaven, what is heaven like to her? I wonder if heaven is located somewhere amidst the lofty, puffy clouds. In regards to her father's illness, how does she think God can make her father get well? What is the mechanism by which a personified God can heal? Perhaps I am being too analytical and overly rigorous with my questions about a spiritual act, and that of an eight-year-old at that.

Perhaps I should, instead, turn the questions toward me, asking how I would answer the same questions about a Buddhist girl "praying" before the Buddha or a bodhisattva for the same kind of wish? The image that immediately crops up in my mind is of a girl of about twelve and her mother whom I saw at a pagoda in Rangoon, Burma, a number of years ago. The girl is wearing a large, red fresh flower in her hair and has on traditional apparel. She sits with her mother on a marble floor of a spacious area in front of Buddha images that are several meters in height. She holds a bouquet of flowers held upright between the palms of hands in a gesture of reverence. She sits with her legs folded but thrown out to her side, a style common in her country as well as in Thailand. Her eyes appear closed, and her head is slightly bowed down toward the Buddha images. She stays in that posture for what seems like several minutes; her mother does the same. I don't know, of course, what is going on inside, but she is certainly not meditating.

I believe this is an important point to make here, for Buddhists are stereotypically seen to only meditate. However, the vast majority of lay Buddhists in Asia primarily "pray" or express themselves devotionally, during which they give thanks but also petition for one thing or another of worldly nature. While panoply of Bodhisattvas such as Avalokiteshvara and Kshitigarbha serve as objects of these earthly petitions in Mahayana Buddhist countries of East Asia, the Shakyamuni Buddha is the primary object of devotion in the Theravada societies of Southeast Asia.

Shakyamuni Buddha, then, is the object of her request. The huge images of the Buddha in his meditation pose sit in front of her. Supposing she too is asking for her father's early recovery from an illness, I wonder what kind of image she holds of the Buddha. Would that image in her mind be the tranquil, meditative Buddha, or the handsome, gallant prince Siddhartha, who boldly went off to seek truth, or the image of some "fatherly figure" from her life experience? More than likely, her image is amorphous, as an amalgamation of the images mentioned above, and more. However way she may conceive of the Buddha, she must feel a satisfying level of comfort with the Buddha for such a deeply personal and devotional act to hold any sense of meaning.

While we see similarities between these two girls, I believe that the act of Christian prayer entails one quality that is virtually absent in the Buddhist devotional form: an interaction with the ultimate, in other words, God. The Christian prayer is a two-way communication, a conversation with God. In contrast, there is virtually no sense of the Burmese girl having a conversation with the Buddha. To her Buddha may answer her prayers for better crop or physical healing, but I would be very surprised if she expected to interact with Buddha on a personal level, whereby, for example, she experienced a spiritual conversation with him. On the other hand, Megan (the American Christian girl), in her prayers would talk with her God in a much more personal way. She may even barter or negotiate with him, offering to be a "good girl" if only God can cure her father of his illness. God appears more willing to listen to her needs and to respond on an individual basis. God at this level is more like a caring uncle who is willing to listen and talk with her.

Now, this leads me to another character of Christian prayer that I believe plays a vital role in making Christian spirituality more accessible to "ordinary" people. The prayer as I have described above does not involve an inward apprehension of the mystical divine presence. Most prayers are not mystical, and it would be going too far to claim mystical experience for ordinary prayer. Like Megan, prayers seek God above and not within. This, in fact, does distinguish Megan's prayer from Buddhist meditation, which most people agree involves some form of "mystical experience." It is precisely this point that gives some conservative Buddhists the necessary proof of the "superior" nature of Buddhist soteriology over that of Christianity. I shall return to this Buddhist claim later, but I wish to point out here that this is also the reason for the less accessible nature of mainstream Buddhist spirituality to ordinary folk. In this respect, Christian prayer at whatever level, certainly including Megan's, is more effective in being inclusive and allowing more people to be "connected" to mainstream Christian spirituality. Megan's prayers are carried out in very ordinary circumstances (at home before going to bed) with real human concern (father's illness). I believe this ability of prayer to affirm the mundane and to lead the seekers to deeper levels of Christian spirituality has been a real asset to Christianity.

I am afraid that I cannot say the same for meditation. Its aim has been to be much more disengaged from the mundane, thus less accessible to ordinary Buddhists in Asia (though interestingly the opposite may be the case in contemporary West, where meditation, as presented, is the primary appeal of Buddhism). One of the reasons for meditation's disengagement from mundane concerns (e.g., Megan's concern for her father's illness) is that they are regarded as the very source of suffering (attachment to a person). This samsaric (cycle of births and deaths) existence needs to be transcended through personal cultivation in which meditation plays a key role. However, such meditation practices with extremely lofty mystical goals were not easily accessible to ordinary Buddhists.

This vacuum has come to be filled with such "devotional practices" as sutra chanting, making offerings of flowers, lanterns, or food, and "prayers" (e.g., Burmese girl described above). However, from the mainstream monastic Buddhist view these practices are viewed as secondary or, at best, provisional. Nevertheless, it is these that the majority of lay Buddhists engage in on a daily basis. Allow me here to elaborate on some examples of what I mean by "prayer."

It is customary for Buddhist sutra chanting to include a "prayer of blessing" called, "the verse for transferring of merit to others." For example, in my own Jodo Shinshu tradition, virtually every sutra chanting ends with the following verse:

> *Gan ni shi ku do ku* (May this merit-virtue)
> *Byo do se is-sai* (Be shared equally with all beings.)
> *Do hotsu bo da-i shin* (May we together awaken the Bodhi Mind,)
> *Ou jou an raku koku* (And be born in the realm of Serenity and Joy.)

This verse is taken from the writing of a seventh-century Chinese master, Shantao. Since everyone, including children, participates in the sutra chanting at religious services, far more people than the small number of priests take part in this "prayer of blessing."

A similar but even more popular form of prayer of blessing called the "Golden Chain" (one that was composed in Hawaii in the early part of the twentieth century) is recited at religious services, particularly when youths and young adults are in attendance.

Golden Chain— II
  I am a link in the Buddha's golden chain of love that stretches around the world. I must keep my link bright and strong.
  I will be kind and gentle to every living being and protect all who are weaker than myself.
  I will try to think pure and beautiful thoughts, to say pure and beautiful words, and to do pure and beautiful deeds, knowing on what I do now depends not only my happiness, but also that of others.
  May every link in the Buddha's golden chain of love become bright and strong, and may we all attain perfect peace.

Particularly the last stanza expresses the Bodhisattva spirit of wishing all beings to realize the ultimate goal of all Buddhists, that is, nirvana or Buddhahood. I personally have regarded this last stanza and the previously cited "verse for merit transference" as my Buddhist prayer for all living beings.

If what I have discussed above can be regarded as "prayers of blessing," what I am about to share can be seen as "prayers of petition," on the same order as that of Megan's prayer for her father to get well. Scholars may regard them as self-serving and, technically, not religious, but I doubt we can easily dismiss them, especially when the "petitioners" are carrying them out within their respective religious framework (God, Buddha, Bodhisattva, etc.) and at formally recognized settings (Buddhist temples, etc.), as we shall see.

As I write this on January 2 here in Japan, the temples are inundated with people who gather for the annual New Year's visits (*hatsu-mode*). It is estimated that almost half of the Japanese population of 125 million people pay visits to Buddhist temples or Shinto shrines on the first three days of the New Year. What motivates so many people to fight the huge crowds to participate, especially when most of them never go to temples or shrines the rest of the year? The primary motivation can be categorized as "prayers of petition." In general, they pray for "a safe, healthy and prosperous" New Year. Of course, there are numerous more specific prayers such as for their loved ones or themselves to recover from illness, to enter a college of their choice, or not to lose their job or business in the current bad economy. On one level these motivations seem "worldly" and petitionary. None is more so than the common scene of people gathered around incense burners fanning the incense smoke onto parts of their body needing fixing or improvement. Some see the need for "purification" of their persistent back pain, of their head to do better on examinations, or of their legs to look thinner for cosmetic purpose.

Perhaps for many these actions are done with a light-hearted expectation, for they "really" don't think that they work, but do it out of custom and just in case it works! However, there are others whose motivations are serious and compelling. A woman in her late seventies suffering from cancer stands in front of the image of Kannon-sama (Avalokiteshvara). All medical treatments have failed and she is told that she has perhaps one year to live. She places her palms together out of genuine feeling of reverence to the Kannon. She expresses her deeply felt gratitude for the wonderful family she feels she has been blessed with — a caring and devoted husband, and three grown children with wonderful families of their own. She is grateful for the fact that she was able to work at a meaningful job for twenty years at a time when it was not fashionable for women with families to do so. She has no regrets. However, she wants to live a little longer. She would like to be able to see all her family again at the next New Year's family gathering. So, after her expressions of appreciation about her life, she petitions Kannon-sama for her cancer to slow down so as to be able to visit the same temple next New Year. Then, adding to her grateful and petitionary thoughts, she also asks for the compassion of Kannon-sama so that when she has to go, she would be embraced and protected. She has not arrived at a doctrinal Buddhist understanding of what happens to her after death, but she would be satisfied as long as she is assured that she "would be all right." This anxiety about "being all right" is partially consoled because she is confident that her family would regularly pay visits to her grave, where her ashes would be interred. She also knows that her family would also take good care of the Buddhist altar at home (where her Buddhist name would be displayed along with her photo) by regularly lighting the incense and candles with offerings of flowers and, at times, her favorite food.

This elderly lady is actually my projection of what probably was going on in the mind of someone I have come to know intimately, my mother-in-law. She went to the temple today, and I surmised what probably took place. I chose to talk about her because it is real (and personal for me) and representative of what actually happens. There are thousands of people like her (and millions like the ordinary *hatsu-mode* visitors discussed above) at Buddhist temples throughout the world. And they equally represent the living Buddhist traditions of today along with the meditating monks and nuns. Perhaps, therefore, meditation should not readily be considered the Buddhist counterpart to Christian prayer, for, as seen above, "prayer" in its many forms is very much carried out and by a majority of people who regard themselves as Buddhists.

I must at this point qualify my somewhat critical comments concerning Buddhist mediation (especially given my Japanese Pure Land background, known for its antimeditation stance). I am in no way categorically condemning meditation, for I too practice an elementary form of Theravada *vipassana* meditation learned during my monastic stint in a Thai monastery in 1970. What I object to is the attitude that privileges meditation at the expense of other forms of practices, thus contributing to the view that excludes a large number of people from "authentic" Buddhist spirituality. In stark contrast, Christian prayer (at least in its contemporary form) has helped to avoid this Buddhist pitfall.

Now, let me turn to couple of other comments I have about Christian prayer, particularly in its public forms (as opposed to the private ones discussed so far). I could not help but take note of the invocation at the U.S. president's inaugural ceremony, where the Christian minister sought God's guidance in helping President George W. Bush to carry out his duties and responsibilities as president. Then the minister invoked God's help for Vice-President Dick Cheney as well as for the wives of these new leaders. I wondered whether God is able to render help to such specific people when there were over six billion people in the world! I don't mean to make light of this, for I realize that such an invocation holds profound spiritual and theological meaning for those involved and that this has become an indelible part of our political liturgy. But on a gut-level reaction for this Buddhist, I see a tinge of self-serving quality about the way in which God was being solicited. It seems to me that God is concerned with all people (and from a Buddhist perspective, all beings) and is, thus, beyond being connected to a specific nation or individuals.

Perhaps my uneasiness was triggered by the obvious manifestation of "civil religion" in action and the seemingly undermining of the principle of separation of state and religion at this presidential inauguration as well as those that have preceded it. The self-serving nature of public prayer is not confined to important political events but is especially glaring in athletic games where prayers (in the forms of thanksgiving and invocation) often serve one's own team at the expense of the other. I often wonder, "Does God really take sides?"

The second observation that I have of public prayers, especially of the thanksgiving variety, is God's monopoly on the credits. Everything worth being thankful for is attributed to God. I can understand this, given the role of God as the maker of all things seen and unseen, but from a Buddhist view it seems that more credits are warranted for the deserving people, other living beings, plants, or unseen conditions. When one gives thanks to God for the food we are about to partake, shouldn't there be thanks given also to the cow, fish, or broccoli whose lives we took for our benefit? Yes, God created them, but they made the real sacrifice. I realize that for some Christians God represents all, so that in giving thanks to God, one is inherently thanking all the creatures and living things. My reticence with acknowledging only God stems from the Buddhist view that does not see Buddha as a creator. We therefore give thanks to him for showing us the way to liberation but not necessarily for the bounty bestowed us.

I regret that the pressures of time have permitted me to present only an impressionistic essay, not a researched article as I had hoped. But perhaps such an impressionistic essay may be a more accurate and honest representation of my views on the topic of Christian prayer (in a comparative framework that includes Buddhist prayer and meditation). In reflecting again on what I have learned from jotting down my thoughts on this topic, I am left with the image of Megan, which I would still like to hold up as my paradigmatic Christian prayer: conversational, personal, and hopeful.

Jesus Prayer and the Nembutsu

Taitetsu Unno
Smith College

A S A SHIN BUDDHIST of the Pure Land tradition, I find the practice of Jesus Prayer in Eastern Orthodox Christianity fascinating, because so much of it resonates with my own experience in the saying of Nembutsu or the Name — NAMU-AMIDA-BUTSU.[1] One calls on the Name of Jesus, and the other on the Name of Amida, the Buddha of Immeasurable Light and Life. Both may be called the "Way of the Name."[2] Some appreciation of the Jesus Prayer may help us understand the depth of Nembutsu experience, for the similarities are striking, but there are also fundamental differences.

We begin with four definitions of prayer as given by the Orthodox scholar Kallistos Ware.[3] The first may be called *external prayer,* which includes some form of verbally addressing God, including petitions for favors to be granted. Second is prayer understood simply as *standing before God.* Here there is only silence, negating all discursive activities. In both of these cases the focus is on the human and not on the divine.

In Buddhist terms these two forms of prayer are dualistic, the subject standing apart from the object and the act centered on the human subject. In Pure Land language both are acts of self-power. In the case of Nembutsu it may also begin as a self-generated act, but it must be superseded. True prayer, as we shall see, is nondualistic with the initiative coming from the side of the divine. In Pure Land terms it is the manifestation of the working of Other Power.

Buddhist meditative practice may also begin in a dualistic mode with personal benefits as the goal, but ultimately it becomes a nondualistic experience, whereby conceptual distinctions of subject and object disappear, so that a deeper reality is realized. The Soto Zen teacher Kosho Uchiyama sums up this awareness:[4]

> In our zazen, it is precisely at the point where our small, foolish self remains unsatisfied, or completely bewildered, that immeasurable natural life beyond the thought of the self functions. It is precisely at the point where we become completely lost that life operates and the power of Buddha is realized.

The third and fourth definitions of prayer, based on Saint Gregory of Sinai, highlight the core experience in Jesus Prayer. The third sense of prayer, according to Ware, is an *inner act*. In his words, "True inner prayer is to stop talking and to listen to the wordless voice of God within our heart; it is to cease doing things on our own, and to enter into the action of God."[5] Here, silence is not mere silence but the openness to hear the wordless voice of God. The initiative comes from the divine: "I have been crucified with Christ and I no longer live, but Christ lives in me" (Gal. 2:20) and "He must become greater, I must become less" (John 3:30).

Fourth is prayer as *"the manifestation of Baptism,"* not baptism as a ritual act but as the embodying of the divine. This is the state of grace that is brought "to the point of full spiritual perception and conscious awareness when we experience and feel the activity of the Spirit directly and immediately."[6]

These two connotations of prayer may be helpful in understanding the writings of Shinran, the founder of Shin Buddhism, who lived in thirteenth-century Japan.[7] The English translations of his works, coming from an entirely different cultural tradition and written in an alien language, sometimes defy easy comprehension. To take one important example, Shinran states at the beginning of the Chapter of Practice in his major opus, translated as "True Teaching, Practice, and Realization of the Pure Land Way," as follows:[8]

> The great practice is to say the Name of the Tathagata of unhindered light. This practice, embodying all good acts and possessing all roots of virtue, is perfect and most rapid in bringing them to fullness. It is the treasure ocean of virtues that is suchness of true reality. For this reason, it is called great practice. This practice arises from the Vow of great compassion.

Keeping in mind the Jesus Prayer, the meaning of this pronouncement becomes clear. The saying of Nembutsu, the Name of Tathagata or Buddha, is neither a petitionary act nor the result of human calculation (*hakarai*). Rather, "this practice arises from the Vow of great compassion." That is, the source of recitative Nembutsu is suggested by the adjective "great," denoting the Buddha of Immeasurable Light and Life, whose "practice" or activity enables the small-minded to set aside the ego-self even for the moment. Thus, great practice means the salvific act of the Buddha coming through in the intoning of Nembutsu.

Since it is the Buddha's activity being brought to realization in a person, each saying of the Name immediately brings to fullness "all good acts and all roots of virtue." In general Buddhism this is the realization of suchness (*tathata*) or true reality, metaphorically expressed here as the "treasure ocean of virtues." The revolutionary nature of Shinran's teaching made this realization available to anyone who invokes the Name. It changed the course of Japanese Buddhism, for it meant that all those excluded from the Buddhist monastic path in the thirteenth century could now achieve liberation and freedom. Heretofore excluded were hunters, butchers, fishermen, peasants, merchants, and women of all classes.

In sum, the saying of Nembutsu is basically the calling from the Buddha Amida. Hence, I translate the Nembutsu as the Name-that-calls. A lay Buddhist expressed this as follows:[9]

> Although the voice that calls
> NAMU-AMIDA-BUTSU is mine,
> It is the voice of Oya-sama calling me,
> "Come as you are!"

Oya-sama is a term of intimacy when referring to one's mother or father and in some cases both parents together. It is interesting to note that D. T. Suzuki, who first translated Shinran's opus into English, rendered the original term for Amida Buddha's Primal Vow (*purvapranidhana* in Sanskrit, or *hongan* in Japanese) as "Prayer."[10] While linguistically idiosyncratic, it conveys the ultimate significance of the Primal Vow as the deep prayer that all beings, regardless of class, gender, occupation, or moral culpability, may attain liberation and freedom from karmic bondage. He also translated *gyo* not as the usual "practice" but as "Living." The Prayer of boundless compassion enfolds us in our everyday life; thus, Living itself where we contend with our ego-self becomes the basic practice for Shin Buddhists.

Now, the ultimate goal of Orthodox prayer, according to Ware, is to "Become what you are,"[11] not simply on the human level but by discovering grace that works within each person. The purpose of Nembutsu practice is also to become truly human by living NAMU-AMIDA-BUTSU, such that a finite being (NAMU) — limited, imperfect, fallible, vulnerable and mortal — realizes itself within the bosom of boundless compassion (AMIDA-BUTSU). Such a life, characterized by humility, gratitude and quiet confidence, is brought to reality in the saying of Nembutsu. Saichi, a Myokonin — those rare and simple but profound Shin faithfuls — expressed it thusly:[12]

> When you catch a cold,
> you can't stop coughing.
> Saichi has caught the cold of Buddha Dharma —
> and can't stop coughing,
> coughing Namu-amida-butsu

The appeal and effectiveness of Jesus Prayer, according to the Orthodox tradition, is ascribed to four factors: simplicity and flexibility, completeness, power of Name as such, and spiritual discipline of persistent repetition. Here again we see comparable points made about the saying of Nembutsu with the exception of the fourth, spiritual discipline.

Honen, Shinran's teacher, who first established an independent Pure Land School in 1175 C.E., advocated Nembutsu practice as an alternative to the complex, rigorous practices of his own Tendai Buddhism, to which he had devoted his whole life. He proclaimed two qualities of Nembutsu as responding to the spiritual hunger of his time: extreme simplicity and unequalled superiority. Simplicity because the saying of Nembutsu could be practiced anywhere, any time, by anyone; and superiority because the attainment of supreme enlightenment has already been accomplished by the working of the Primal Vow. In experiential terms that which is simple, in contrast to surface complexity, cuts deep, deep into the depth of life itself. In so doing it also expands endlessly to embrace all of life, animate and inanimate.

The Pure Land teachers also understood the Vow not simply as the deep wish that all beings attain supreme enlightenment but also as containing the power to make it an actuality. In fact, the Name or Nembutsu contains the forty-eight Vows of Amida fulfilled as the culmination and completion of the bodhisattva ideal.[13] As such, the Name itself is the Buddha incarnate in our world; it has no objective referent beyond it. Thus the preferred object of Shin devotional worship is not the statue or painting of Amida Buddha but the Name, NAMU-AMIDA-BUTSU, written on a scroll and placed on the altar.

Regarding spiritual discipline, recitative Nembutsu was considered a religious practice down through the centuries since the beginning of Pure Land Buddhism in the first century C.E. in India, but it was rejected as a self-power activity by Shinran. Instead, he saw the Nembutsu as evidence of the working of Amida in the heart and mind of a person here and now. Thus, a single utterance of the Name would be sufficient; in fact, just the thought of such a voicing would suffice. In his words, "When the thought of saying the Nembutsu erupts from deep within, having entrusted ourselves to the inconceivable power of Amida's vow which saves us, enabling us to be born in the Pure Land, we receive at that very moment the ultimate benefit of being grasped never to be abandoned."[14] Repetition as a spiritual discipline is unnecessary because the decisive moment of spiritual awakening is a matter of here and now. The Jesus Prayer also has a similar emphasis, yet it encourages repetition and, for the monks, the training of the body, including breathing exercises.[15]

The here and now is basic, because the Primal Vow of Amida breaks through conventional, linear time. The timeless penetrates through time at every instant. This is called the one-thought moment of spiritual awakening. In the words of Shinran, "One thought-moment is time at its ultimate limit, where the realization of shinjin takes place."[16] Shinjin is the awakening to the Primal Vow becoming manifest in one's life, whereby all doubts vanish and true entrusting appears. This one-thought moment is vocalized by the saying of Name, pouring out spontaneously as a total and joyful compliance with the working of boundless compassion.

Orthodox prayer warns against creating visual images, visions, or forms, as enticements to delusion.[17] The full power of the Jesus Prayer is felt when one abandons all visual concepts and simply feels God's presence. Shin Buddhism also negates visualization of any form, although it was common practice in the long history of the Pure Land movement in India, China, Korean, and Japan prior to Shinran.

Such practices, for example, are itemized in the Contemplation Sutra, one of the three main scriptures of Pure Land Buddhism, compiled around the fourth century C.E. probably in Central Asia or China.[18] These practices include thirteen methods of contemplation, centered on the setting sun, water, earth, jeweled trees, jeweled ponds, jeweled pavilions, jeweled dais, all in the Pure Land, Buddha images, Amida, Avalokitesvara, Mahasthamaprapta, and so on. Although these forms of visualizations must have been practiced at various times, Pure Land masters agreed that they were preliminaries to its ultimate message noted at the very end: A single saying of Nembutsu assures salvation and enlightenment even to a person on the deathbed.

The consequence of Jesus Prayer is said to be twofold: First, it transforms one's relationship with the world, which is seen as being infused with God's presence; and second, it changes a person's relationship with other people.[19] In brief, Jesus Prayer is world-affirming, which is also the case in Shin Buddhism. The two are also found in living the Nembutsu, although expressed with a different sensitivity. Ichitaro, another Myokonin, states: "The Land of Bliss is found everywhere. On a vegetable leaf, On a blade of grass. On a sardine. Without saying whether a thing is good or bad, if you sense the working of Amida in and on each thing, this is the truth freed of the good and bad of things. All good and bad are the products of one's thoughts."[20] When we see a thing and judge it as good or bad, we are basing our view on a self-centered human perspective. When we see the world in the light of boundless compassion, the Land of Bliss or Pure Land can be found everywhere.

Such an awareness makes us keenly sensitive not only to other human beings but to all living things. Thus, Ichitaro on another occasion remarks: "True entrusting means that you're able to truly relate to another being. Not only human beings but with plants and animals. Even those things that cannot speak, you're able to hear their feelings. Namu-amida-butsu."[21] Such a worldview is based on the Buddhist understanding of the vast network of interconnectedness and interdependence that one comes to acknowledge in becoming liberated from the ego-self.

In spite of the striking parallels in Nembutsu practice and Jesus Prayer, fundamental differences exist reflecting the respective histories of Buddhism and Christianity. Among them, perhaps the most important is the treatment of sin, evil, blind passion, darkness, and ignorance (*avidya*).

The Art of Prayer: An Orthodox Anthology, an excellent sourcebook for Jesus Prayer, devotes a major section underscoring the cleavage between good and evil passions, grace and sin, God and Satan, life and death, the latter to be "hated, trampled on, rejected."[22] This duality is repeatedly emphasized, such as in the following passage: "Sin is now driven out from its stronghold and goodness takes its place, while the strength of sin is shattered and dispersed. 'Grace and sin do not dwell together in the mind,' says St. Diadochos, 'but before baptism grace incites the soul to goodness from without, while Satan lurks in its depth, endeavouring to bar all the doors of righteousness in the mind; from the very moment that we are reborn the devil remains outside and grace dwells within.'"[23] I don't know how this relates to Romans 5:20, "Where sin increased, grace abounded all the more," and Martin Luther's *simul iustus et peccator,* but it presents a sharp contrast to Shinran, who sees the raison d'être of boundless compassion to be the transformation of evil into good, sin into virtue, death into life. To negate evil, sin, and death means to deny a part of one's reality; to affirm them through transformation means to make one's life complete and whole.

This transformation of the negative into the positive is summed up in the phrase "bits of rubble are transformed into gold." Shinran's favorite metaphor for transformation is that of ice into water:[24]

> Through the benefit of the unhindered light,
> We realize shinjin of vast, majestic virtues,
> And the ice of our blind passions necessarily melts.
> Immediately becoming water of enlightenment.
> Obstructions of karmic evil turn into virtues;
> It is like the relation of ice and water;
> The more the ice, the more the water;
> The more the obstructions, the more the virtues.

The philosophical basis of this transformation is rooted in the Buddhist worldview that sees impermanence, flux, and change as elemental and all phenomenal reality as devoid or empty of enduring essence (*sunyata*). Yet human ignorance is such that we cling to things and trap ourselves in anger, jealousy, fear, insecurities, addictions. But this foolish being undergoes transformation into its opposite, a process inherent in nature itself, called "made to become so" by itself and for itself. According to Shinran, "'To be made to become so' means that without the practicer's calculation in any way whatsoever, all his past, present, and future evil karma is transformed into the highest good. To be transformed means the evil karma without being nullified and eradicated is made into the highest good, just as all river waters, upon entering the great ocean, immediately become ocean water."[25] This transformation results spontaneously from the working of Other Power that is beyond conceptual understanding. It should not be confused with the power of positive thinking or some form of creative therapy.

The challenge to Shin Buddhists is to awaken to this compassionate working of the Buddha of Immeasurable Light and Life not by strenuous repetition of the Name but by awakening to its origin and import for oneself. This requires effort and dedication to a process called deep hearing (*monpo*), which consists of four aspects that are interrelated and interconnected. First is receptivity to the teaching of the Name-that-calls. Second is unfolding awareness of its truth in one's life, consisting of its two aspects: boundless compassion and karmic bondage. Third is the growing sensitivity to the interplay of light and darkness, boundless compassion and blind passion, expanding horizon and diminishing self-enclosure. Fourth is awakening to the call of Amida that works a miraculous transformation — negative into positive, darkness into luminosity, and blind passion into the very content of supreme enlightenment.

Notes

1. For Jesus Prayer, see *The Way of the Pilgrim,* 2d ed., trans. R. M. French (New York: Harper, 1954), and for the Nembutsu, see the author's *Tannisho: A Shin Buddhist Classic,* 2d rev. ed. (Honolulu: Buddhist Study Center Press, 1996), 61–62.

2. *On the Invocation of the Name of Jesus* by a Monk of the Eastern Church (London: Fellowship of St. Alban and St. Sergius, no date), i.

3. Kallistos Ware, "The Power of the Name: The Function of the Jesus Prayer," *Cross Currents* 24, no. 2–3 (Summer-Fall 1974): 184–203. See also Foreword by Kallistos Ware, *The Jesus Prayer* (Crestwood, N.Y.: St. Valdimir's Seminary Press, 1987) and *The Art of Prayer: An Orthodox Anthology,* comp. Igunen Chariton (London: Faber and Faber, 1966).

4. Kosho Uchiyama, *Opening the Hand of Thought: Approach to Zen* (New York: Penguin, 1993), 61.

5. Ware, "The Power of the Name," 185.

6. Ibid., 186.

7. *The Collected Works of Shinran,* trans. Dennis Hirota, et al. (Kyoto: Jodo Shinshu Hongwanji-ha, 1997), vols. 1 and 2 (hereafter CW I and II).

8. CW I, 13.

9. *Dharma Treasures: Spiritual Insights from Hawaii's Shin Buddhist Pioneers,* ed. Tatsuo Muneto (Honolulu: Buddhist Study Center, 1997), 35.

10. See *The Kyogyoshinsho: The Collection of Passages Expounding the True Teaching, Living, Faith, and Realization of the Pure Land* (Kyoto: Shinshu Otani-ha, 1973).

11. Ware, "The Power of the Name," 186.

12. *Myokonin Asahara Saichi shu* (Collected Poems of Saishi the Myokonin), ed. D. T. Suzuki (Tokyo: Shunjusha, 1967), 147.

13. For the forty-eight vows, see the translation from the Chinese by Luis Gomez, *The Land of Bliss: The Paradise of the Buddha of Measureless Light* (Honolulu: University of Hawai'i Press; and Kyoto: Higashi Honganji Shinshu Otani-ha, 1996).

14. *Tannisho: A Shin Buddhist Classic,* tr. Taitetsu Unno (Honolulu: Buddhist Study Center Press, 1996), 4.

15. In Shin Buddhism the natural rhythm of the body, including proper breathing, is realized by virtue of the thirty-third Vow of Amida, which ensures suppleness, flexibility, and openness of the body and mind.

16. CW I, 474.

17. *The Art of Prayer,* 100–101.

18. For this sutra, see English translation by Hisao Inagaki, *The Three Pure Land Sutras* (Berkeley, Calif.: Numata Center for Buddhist Research and Publication, 1995).

19. Ware, "The Power of the Name," 199–200.

20. Tetsuo Unno, *Jodoshinshu Buddhism* (South San Francisco: Heian International, 1980), 12.

21. Quoted in my *River of Fire, River of Water: An Introduction to the Pure Land Tradition of Shin Buddhism* (New York: Doubleday, 1998), 121.

22. *The Art of Prayer,* 140.

23. Ibid., 172.

24. CW I, 371.

25. CW I, 453.

Buddhist Prayer? A Reflection

MAHINDA DEEGALLE

Bath Spa University College

"PRAYER" IS NOT a traditional Buddhist term found either within the Theravāda or Mahāyāna Buddhist vocabulary. In the modern world, however, in inter-religious dialogue and in thematic studies in comparative religion, more scholars and practitioners are searching for visible parallels and common grounds both in doctrine and practice among the world religions. As it is the case with this edited volume, the two editors — Professors Rita M. Gross and Terry Muck — have identified prayer as one of the most important religious practices within the Christian traditions that can be seen, examined, analyzed, and critiqued from a variety of Buddhist perspectives.

The following examination is a modest attempt to understand Christian notions of prayer from a Theravāda Buddhist perspective of Sri Lanka. However, not restricting my exploration to the Theravāda tradition, I plan to examine some Buddhist ritual practices that can be included in the category of prayer. This exploration will go against the overwhelming popular consensus among Theravāda Buddhists that they do not have forms of prayer within their religious practices and traditions. To explore the possibility of having categories of prayer within the lives of Theravāda Buddhists, I will examine both *emic* and *etic* understandings of prayer within Sri Lankan Buddhist society. I will consider Theravāda notions of worship and mindful practices associated with meals within the Theravāda and Sōtō Zen Buddhist traditions. I will also examine the genre of petitions called *kannalavva* used by Buddhist shamans in Sri Lanka whose role within the Buddhist pantheon of Sri Lanka is to serve the cult of popular deities. As anthropological literature has shown, within the Sinhala

Buddhist popular practices, the *kannalavva* genre of texts are used as "functional prayers." Finally, the examination of the *Liberating Prayer* within the New Kadampa Tradition shows that modern Western Buddhists have adopted the functional role of Christian prayer as a result of being unable to transcend the Christian heritage of the West.

Modern Interpreters of Prayer

Reginald Stephen Copleston, bishop of Colombo, in his magnum opus *Buddhism: Primitive and Present* (1908), made a short comment on our topic — prayer — from an *etic* (outsider) perspective:

> Of prayer, primitive Buddhism knows nothing. There is no room for prayer, properly so called, in a system which admits no supreme God, nor any being essentially and permanently superior to man. The monk, who claims that the gods do homage to him, cannot pray; and whatever petition a man may offer to Brahma, Indra, or other deities, is only the petition of one who for the time is out of office to one who is in a position to assist him. But in modern Buddhism the instinct of prayer finds frequent expression, and is probably the more genuine the less it rests on theory.

Here Copleston had rightly noted the tensions that exist with regard to prayer within the Sri Lankan Theravāda Buddhism with which he was familiar. From a strictly canonical perspective, early forms of Buddhism, which Copleston identified as "primitive Buddhism," had no room for prayer — petitions directed to a Supreme Being — as understood in the prayers within the Christian traditions. As Pāli canonical Buddhism maintains, if human beings have the potential to realize the ultimate goal — *nibbāna* — without the assistance of another person, there is no need to rely on a supreme being and make petitions to that authority. The Buddhist monk or nun as a full member of the Buddhist community cannot rely on petitions. He or she should rely on oneself for the ultimate liberation from suffering. The monk or nun cannot attain liberation through prayer but instead he or she has to practice meditation and realize the truth within him or herself. In the process of adaptation of that canonical soteriological message into the Buddhist societies of South and Southeast Asia and its growth and its translation into a variety of popular religious beliefs and practices within those societies, as Copleston noted, there had been "the instinct of prayer"; furthermore, a scholar can examine and study as possible candidates for Buddhist forms of prayer its "frequent expression" in various forms within modern Buddhist societies.

Copleston did not forget to provide a gloss to his previous comment on the nature of Buddhist prayer:

> The theory is two-fold. In some cases it is held that the deities who control earthly affairs are accessible to petition, just as kings are. The other view, more strictly Buddhist, is this: that merit, one's own or that of another, and especially that of the Buddha, can be brought to bear on one's own needs or on those of others. This may be called the theory, that wishes, when supported by merit, are efficacious.[1]

Thus Copleston identified two dimensions of Buddhist religiosity in twentieth-century Sri Lanka. One important pragmatic and functional dimension of Sri Lankan Theravāda Buddhism accepts the efficacy of various minor deities in the divine pantheon of popular Buddhism; they will listen to Buddhist devotees' petitions and will take care of mundane business by granting good health, success, and prosperity. Another important religious and Buddhist dimension is the Buddhist's heavy reliance of one's own meritorious deeds. While the latter notion has the backing of canonical Buddhism that one's good or bad actions have power over the doer, the former belief is a concession made within the social and religious development of the country allowing human beings to rely on someone's help at times of trouble as a psychological solace.

Against this twentieth-century scholarly argument for the existence of certain forms of prayer within Sri Lankan Buddhist society, it would be valuable also to pay attention to *emic* (insider) understanding of the role of prayer within Sri Lankan Buddhist life. The Theravāda Buddhist reformer Anagārika Dharmapāla (1864–1933) explains the role of prayer within Theravāda Buddhism as follows. Dharmapāla helps us understand the way that some traditional Buddhists have been vocal in showing a "difference" between Buddhist and Christian religious practices:

Prayer to a God is not possible for a Buddhist, but he can make what is called a "sacca kiriya" an appeal to truth. "If the work that I am doing is good then let help come to me, and if the work that I am doing is good help will surely come." And help came four days after we were threatened by the landlord. Not from the Buddhists of Asia, but from Mrs. T. R. Foster of Honolulu.... My will prayer for the fulfillment of my cherished desires for the resuscitation of Buddhism in the land of its birth after 2500 years of its foundation was answered.[2]

Here Dharmapāla denies the existence of the notion of prayer within Theravāda Buddhism. However, he introduces an alternative practice to talk about the notion of prayer. He explains his aspirations for the revival of Buddhism in India and Sri Lanka under the British Government and Christian dominance as an act of *saccakiriya* (truth). He will benefit from his aspirations because those aspirations are inherently good — good aspirations lead to good results. Dharmapāla thus rejects the notion of prayer as an outside imposition on Buddhists and he explains his activities using the indigenous category of *saccakiriya*. Dharmapāla further comments:

Happiness could be realized here not by sacrificing to the gods, and praying to get possessions, but in ceaseless activity in doing good in helping the sick both animals and men....[3]

Dharmpāla has seen that a prayer made with the intention of material benefit is useless. He promotes an understanding of active engagement in social welfare activities for the benefit of the masses rather than of being active engagement in prayer. This Buddhist interpretation is important in understanding some Buddhist reactions to the use of the word "prayer" and explaining similar activities using different terms common to Asian traditions.

Prayer within the Sinhala Buddhism

In Sinhala Buddhism,[4] Buddhists use prayers in popular rituals. Specific Sinhala words that are relevant here in understanding the notion of prayer are *kannalavva* ("plaint") and *yādinna* ("prayer"). Gananath Obeyesekere, in his

study of *The Cult of the Goddess Pattini,* gives some texts of *kannalavva* in relation to the study of the cult of Pattini. These *kannalavva* texts include aspects of
petitions contained in the prayer. Indigenous shamans, known as *kapurāla,* who
attend the business related to deities of the Sinhala pantheon such as Viṣṇu and
Kataragama, recite the *kannalavva* texts to make petitions to the divine bodies.
These petitions do not go against Buddhist notions since they are well-conceived
within the Buddhist soteriological path and worldview:

> May you live long [for] five thousand years....May you become a Bud-
> dha...while the *sāsana* of the Buddha and the *sāsana* of the *dēavas* last.
> ...O Sahampati the great [Mahā] Brahma, noble king possessed of great
> spiritual power, who looks upon this isle of Sri Lanka with divine kindness
> and listens to the exhortations made in your name. O Sakra, chief of the
> world of gods, listen to the requests made in your name. O Śrī Viṣṇu pos-
> sessed of great spiritual powers, protector of Sri Lanka and the *sāsana* of
> the Buddha who listens [to us] and benevolently looks on us....O great
> Viṣṇu...most noble king listen to the pleas made by your servant [*gäti*],
> accept our merit and protect us.

After seeking protection from Mahābrahma, Sakra, and Viṣṇu (the protector
of *sāsana* in Sri Lanka), the petition also mention the names of other deities in
the Sinhala pantheon beginning with Śrī Sumana Saman (the guardian deity
of the Adam's Peak), Vibhīṣaṇa, Gaṇeśa, Skanda (the deity of the Kataragama
dēvāle), the seven Pattini goddesses, Śrī Dēvatā Baṇḍāra, Devol, Gini Kurum-
bara, Hūniyan, and the seven Kiri Ammas. Then the petition makes an explicit
practical request:

> I, your servant, have exhorted you...on behalf of all these villagers who
> believe in you so that they may never see or hear of pestilence and plagues
> and disease, and calamities, give them divine protection, save them from
> ritual cursing and curses at Devol shrines, from the evil looks of *dēvatās,*
> from bad times...save them from the dangers, diseases, and sudden
> calamities that may result from divine anger and wrath, from the looks of
> *dēvatās,* from bodily error... [save us] from the misfortune that may have
> already struck us from the nine planets...protect us and help us to thrive

in the fields we hereafter cultivate, in journeys we make, in our trades, in our jobs and professions.

Beyond material success, the petition moves to request intelligence:

> We plead thus that in the future you would obtain for these people... the wisdom of Gaṇeśa... the blessings of Sarasvatī ... Śrī Kāntā's gaze in their houses and fields and gardens.[5]

Inserting the local deities into the divine pantheon, this *kannalavva* gives a clear hierarchy of the divine pantheon in Sinhala Buddhism. Ordinary Sinhalese make plaints of this sort to divine bodies to seek protection for the Buddha's message and for Buddhist establishments in Sri Lanka. As it is here, the plaint is inclusive and contains a whole range of divine bodies within its petition. The Buddhist notion of merit (*puñña*) is also repeated again and again in the petitions and one's good work is given prominence in making the petition. The petitioner always reminds the deity to "listen to the pleas made in your name" and "accept our merit and protect us." While the notion of prayer and the petition dimension are clearly visible in *kannalavva* texts, in the Buddhist services, however, the prayer dimension is rather ambiguous.

FORMS OF PRAYER WITHIN THERAVĀDA AND MAHĀYĀNA BUDDHIST PRACTICES

> Prayer is... for being abundantly fed with Enlightenment.
>
> D. T. Suzuki[6]

In the strict sense of the word, Buddhists may not have prayers in the Christian sense. Nevertheless, there are many mindfulness practices within the Buddhist traditions that come closer to the category of prayer in broader terms. In this section, I plan to demonstrate the nature of mindfulness practices which in some ways function as Buddhist prayers within the Theravāda and Mahāyāna Buddhist traditions.

An age-old practice within Theravāda monasticism is the four recollections at the moment of using the four requisites approved for a Buddhist monastic.

The four requisites approved for a *bhikkhu* (male renouncer) or a *bhikkhunī* (female renouncer) are: (1) robes (*cīvara*), (2) food (*piṇḍapāta*), (3) lodgings (*senāsana*), and (4) medicine (*gilānappaccaya bhesajja*). These four means of support for one's life are known within the Theravāda traditions in Pāli as *catu paccaya*. When a Buddhist monastic uses any of these basic necessities, he or she is expected to practice a mindful meditation on the use of them:

1. *Mindful Practice on Robes*
   With proper consideration, I use the robes only to ward off cold, to ward off heat, to ward off contact with gadflies and mosquitoes, wind, sun and reptiles, and only to cover the private parts.

2. *Mindful Practice on Almsfood*
   With proper consideration, I use the almsfood, not for playing, not for displaying vigor, not for ornamentation, not for adornment, but only for the continuation and sustenance of this body, to keep it unharmed and to help me lead the holy life. Thus I shall destroy the past sensations and not produce new sensations and my life will continue without fault and I shall live at ease.

3. *Mindful Practice on Lodgings*
   With proper consideration, I use the lodgings only to ward off cold, to ward off heat, to ward off contact with gadflies and mosquitoes, wind, sun and reptiles, to avoid the rigors of seasons and other dangers and to take joy in seclusion.

4. *Mindful Practice on Medicine*
   With proper consideration, I use the requisites for the sick and offerings of medicaments, only to ward off painful feelings that have arisen when the body is ill and because freedom from disease is the highest.[7]

A renouncer should always be mindful of using the four requisites and should reflect on the real advantages of them for one's own monastic livelihood. This mindfulness practice is meant to create a positive attitude toward human life and its conditioning. As religious virtuosi, they are not expected to be attached to either sensual attractions or superficial attachments. When the renouncer receives something pleasant, he or she should neither cling to it nor crave for it.

As a person who leads a mindful way of living, the renouncer should be satisfied with whatever he or she receives as the benefits of monastic vocation. The cultivation of mindfulness (*sati*) with respect to the four material supports of human life creates a spiritual atmosphere where the renouncer can lead a simple and unburdensome lifestyle. He or she will not be a burden to the community whether one practices in an urban center or in a forest dwelling.

This mindfulness practice should be cultivated at three stages: before accepting the four requisites, while consuming the requisites, and after finishing the consumption of the requisites. The role of these mindful meditations and prayers is to create a religious and spiritual atmosphere for the monastic so that the ideals of monastic life are well reflected in one's lifestyle. These mindful reflections are not exclusively restricted to Theravāda Buddhist monasticism. In other Buddhist traditions also, one can find similar mindful reflections on the meaning of the monastic life and the activities in the monastery.

In the Zen Buddhist monastic traditions in Japan and Korea, it is common to have meal prayers. Both D. T. Suzuki (1974) and Robert Buswell (1992) have documented the meal recitations of Zen monasteries in Japan and Korea. In September 1999, when I was practicing *zazen* at Zensh-ji, a Sōtō Zen monastery in Nara, Japan, I came across the following meal time prayer. The *roshi* (Zen master) Ichida Kōshi, the head teacher of the monastery, who had spent many years as a teacher at Pioneer Valley Meditation Center in the United States (1974–86), outlined the purpose of the prayer at meals:

> Buddhists, like Christians, often say a grace before meals. The prayer used most often by Zen Buddhists is called *Gokannoge* ("The Prayer of the Five Observations"). This is printed on the envelope which holds your chopsticks. The five observations are blessings for which you give thanks. Following it, on the reverse of the envelope, is a prayer that all sentient beings may attain Buddhahood. A short prayer, with much the same meaning, is said after the meal.

These remarks of the *roshi* well summarize the mindful practices associated with meals within a Zen meditation center in modern Japan and how those practices can be understood in relation to Theravāda practices in understanding the role of prayer within the Buddhist traditions.

Before partaking the meal, the Zen practitioners recite the following five contemplations called *Gokannoge* [8] which I translate here as "The Poem of the Five Contemplations."[9]

> First, we reflect on our work and remember how much we owe the people who bring food.[10]
>
> Second, we reflect how imperfect our virtue is and whether we deserve to receive the food.
>
> Third, we reflect how we can restrain ourselves from eating too much and be detached from various faults such as greed.
>
> Fourth, we reflect that we receive the food as medicine to keep our bodies in good health.
>
> Fifth, we reflect that in order to become enlightened we accept this food.[11]

These five contemplations were introduced in the "Rules of the Eiheiji" (*Eihei-genzenji-shingi*) written by Dogen (1200–1253), the founder of the Sōtō Zen school in Japan, for regulating monastic life in a Zen monastery. While the book contains six chapters which were composed at different times, the third chapter deals exclusively on the "Manners in Eating" (*Fushukuhanpō*). It provides the table manners for the Zen monastery. While these contemplations are recited at communal meals at meditation retreats, they become important reflections that demonstrate the continuity of fundamental Buddhist ideas from Indian Buddhism to Japanese Buddhist spiritual practices. While these meal prayers are explicit in Zen training monasteries, they are not by any means limited exclusively to the Zen monastery alone. What they show is that certain types of contemplative practices which one can identify as "prayers" function in Buddhist monasteries whether they are Theravāda or Mahāyāna. While these meal prayers are visible primarily in Zen monastic practices, nevertheless, other Japanese Buddhist groups also use similar prayers.

In addition to reciting the five comtemplations, before partaking the meal, the practitioners recite the following verse which highlights the purpose of religious life for a Buddhist, a Bodhisattva, and a virtuous human being:

> The first morsel is to destroy all negative actions.
> The second morsel is to practice all good deeds.

> The third morsel is to liberate all sentient beings.
> May the entire world attain the path of Buddhahood.[12]
> I gratefully partake the food (*itadakimasu*).[13]

After the meal is taken, it is customary to conclude the meal with a blessing. It functions as a thanksgiving. It reminds one of one's good intentions and asserts the wish that everyone may reach Buddhahood.

> May this way of feeling be shared by all sentient beings. Together with us may they equally attain to the realization of Buddhahood! Thank you for the lovely meal (*gochisōsama*).[14]

Suzuki's views are useful to place this Zen mindful practice in a proper Buddhist context. He has explained the role of prayer within the Zen tradition in his book *The Training of the Zen Buddhist Monk*. Suzuki writes:

> The life of prayer begins with confession; for prayer, in whatever sense it may be taken, is the expression of an earnest desire which is raised when the devotee feels something lacking in himself and seeks to complete himself either through an outside power or by digging deeper into his own being.... In Buddhist terminology, this means to grow conscious of the heaviness of one's own karma-hindrances.... When the devotee is innerly impelled to become conscious of this, he prays. He may not have any definitive knowledge as regards the objective body to which his prayer is offered.... In Zen Buddhism prayers are offered to all the Buddhas and Bodhisattvas of the past, present, and future....[15]

Here one can observe that some Mahāyāna Buddhists like Suzuki are clear about the role of prayer within their traditions and acknowledge the existence of prayer within Buddhist practices in one form or another. In the study of comparative religion, it is always a problem whether one can use the term "prayer" to explain the religious practices of Buddhists; there is always another frequent question whether one wants to use a different term in order to evade the reality of common and popular religious practices within specific Buddhist traditions. Nevertheless, it clear that the notion of prayer is not completely alien to Buddhists of various Buddhist traditions. As Suzuki writes: "With Zen Buddhists prayer is more in the form of self-reflection and vow or determined will than asking for an outside help in the execution of desires."[16] This spiritual dimension of the Buddhist prayer is a key point that one should not loose sight of in the interpretation of Buddhist prayer.

PRAYER OF A MODERN WESTERN BUDDHIST GROUP

THE *LIBERATING PRAYER* of the New Kadampa Tradition (NKT) is illustrative of the way modern Western Buddhists have gradually adopted the notion of prayer in their adaptation and propagation of Buddhism in the West. The Gelugpa monk Geshe Kelsang Gyatso (b. 1932) founded the New Kadampa Tradition in the United Kingdom in 1991. In 1977, the Foundation for the Preservation of the Mahayana Tradition (FPMT) had invited Geshe Kelsang to the UK and he and his followers declared independence from the FPMT in 1991. With a membership of eight thousand individuals and 370 study centers,[17] the NKT professes an exclusive path in which its members study Buddhist practices only within Geshe Kelsang's teaching lineage; it prohibits mixing NKT practices with those of other Buddhist schools. Against the rejection of the Dalai Lama, the NKT venerates the problematic protector deity Dorje Shugden as a manifestation of the Buddha and the most efficacious protector of Western practitioners.

The following *Liberating Prayer* of the NKT illustrates that some Western Buddhists have consciously thought about the notion of prayer and its role in Buddhist religious life in the modern world. Except for the content of this prayer, it would be hard to find any difference between this Buddhist prayer and a popular Christian prayer:

LIBERATING PRAYER

Praise to Shayamuni Buddha

O Blessed One, Shakyamuni Buddha
Precious treasury of compassion,
Bestower of supreme inner peace,

You, who love all beings without exception,
Are the source of happiness and goodness;
And you guide us to the liberating path,

Your body is a wishfulfilling jewel,
Your speech is supreme, purifying nectar,
And your mind is refuge for all living beings,

With folded hands I turn to you,
Supreme unchanging friend,
I request from the depths of my heart:

Please give me the light of your wisdom,
To dispel the darkness of my mind
And to heal my mental continuum.

Please nourish me with your goodness,
That I in turn may nourish all beings
With an unceasing banquet of delight.

Through your compassionate intention,
Your blessings and virtuous deeds,
And my strong wish to rely upon you,

May all suffering quickly cease
And all happiness and joy be fulfilled;
And may holy Dharma flourish for everyone.[18]

This Tibetan Buddhist prayer is recited daily in NKT centers during the evening *pujā* and it is explicit in its request of asking favors from the Buddha in accomplishing one's goal of helping others as a Buddhist.

CONCLUSIONS

IN THIS PAPER, I have reflected on some *emic* and *etic* views on the notion of prayer when prayer as a religious category is applied to Theravāda Buddhist traditions. I have also included a brief explanation of the role of *kannalavva* which is used almost like a functional prayer within Sinhala Buddhism. With two specific Buddhist examples drawn from the Theravāda and Sōtō Zen Buddhist traditions, I have demonstrated the way meal prayers are organized as contemplative practices for developing mindfulness and as ways of realizing the goals of monastic life within the daily monastic routine. The examination of the *Liberating Prayer* taken from the New Kadampa Tradition shows the way modern Western Buddhists have adopted the functional role of the notion of prayer to their religious lives in interpreting Buddhist ideas and values to the Buddhists who are living now in the West.

NOTES

1. Copleston (1892:269–70).
2. Dharmapāla (1965:747).
3. Dharmapāla (1965:78).
4. For a definition of Sinhala Buddhism, see Deegalle (1997).
5. Obeyesekere (1984).
6. Suzuki (1974:81).
7. A.III.388; Lokuliyana (n.d.:8–9).
8. The Japanese title of this Zen contemplative practice is made up with three Chinese characters. The first Chinese character *go* means "five." The second Chinese character *kan* means "observing," "contemplating," or "realizing" as in *kanjin* where one observes one's original Buddha nature. The third Chinese character *ge* means "verse." It is the Japanese equivalent of Sanskrit *gāthā*. A *ge* or *gāthā* praises the Buddha or restates succinctly the major points in Buddhist doctrine. Thus this genre of prayer can be translated as "verse" or "poem" rather than "prayer."
9. I have translated this mindful practice as the "Five Contemplations." Suzuki (1974:50) mentions them as the "Five Meditations." The *roshi* had translated it as the "Five Observations."
10. Modern printed manuals of Zen Buddhist temples seem to have modified and simplified these ancient five contemplations. The first contemplation in the classical Japanese can be transliterated as *"hitotsu ni wa kō no tasho o hakari, ka no raisho o hakaru."* A modernized version of these five contemplations can be found both in English and in Japanese in *The Five Articles for Buddhist Grace at Meal Time* published by the Soto Sect Headquarters (1960) in Tokyo on January 30, 1960. While p. 1 gives the simplified version of the text, the remaining pages give a commentary on their significance. Also see *http://dx.sakura.ne.jp/~kameno/egokan.html* for the Japanese original that I have used here and for a slightly varied English translation. Another simplified English version is found in item 28 of Sato (1973).

11. See also Suzuki (1974:146) and Buswell (1992:234).

12. See also Suzuki (1974:50, 146).

13. Even in modern Japan, Japanese etiquette involves saying with joined palms *itadakimasu*, a very useful practical polite Japanese expression, before consuming a meal.

14. Saying the polite expression *gochisōsama* (literally: "It was indeed a feast!") at the end of a meal is an important part of Japanese table manners. It would be interesting to examine to what extent Buddhist ideas and practices have been adapted to modern secular Japanese lifestyle.

15. Suzuki (1974:73).

16. Suzuki (1974:73).

17. *http://www.kadampa.net.* This site states variously that there are four hundred and six hundred New Kadampa centers worldwide.

18. *http://www.kadampa.net.org/prayers* gives a special page with prayers recited daily (e.g., *Prayer to Tsongkhapa, A Long Life Prayer for Geshe Kelsang Gyatso,* etc.).

Cited Sources

Buswell, Robert E., Jr. 1992. *The Zen Monastic Experience: Buddhist Practice in Contemporary Korea.* Princeton: Princeton University Press.

Copleston, Reginald Stephen. 1892. *Buddhism: Primitive and Present in Magadha and in Ceylon.* London: Longmans, Green, and Co.

Deegalle, Mahinda. 1997. "A Bibliography on Sinhala Buddhism." *Journal of Buddhist Ethics* 4:216–56.

Dharmapala, Anagarika. 1965. *Return to Righteousness: A Collection of Speeches, Essays and Letters of the Anagarika Dharmapala,* ed. W. P. Ananda Guruge. Colombo: Ministry of Educational and Cultural Affairs.

Lokuliyana, Lionel. n.d. *Catubhāṇavārapāli: The Text of the Four Recitals or the Great Book of Protections.* Trans. Lionel Lokuliyana. Singapore: Ti-sarana Buddhist Association.

Obeyesekere, Gananath. 1984. *The Cult of Goddess Pattini.* Chicago: University of Chicago Press.

Sato, Giei, and Eshin Nishimura. 1973. *Unsui: A Diary of Zen Monastic Life,* ed. Bardwell L. Smith. Honolulu: University of Hawai'i Press.

Soto Sect Headquarters. 1960. *The Five Articles for Buddhist Grace at Meal Time.* Tokyo: The Soto Sect Headquarters.

Suzuki, D. T. 1974. *The Training of the Zen Buddhist Monk.* Berkeley, Calif.: Wingbow Press.

CHRISTIAN RESPONSES

A Christian Response to Buddhist Reflections on Prayer

DONALD W. MITCHELL

Purdue University

IN HIS ESSAY, Kenneth K. Tanaka considers two important elements of Christian prayer when he presents young Megan praying. First is the petitionary element of her prayer, and second is the relational element. Saint John Damascene expresses these same two dimensions in his classical definition of Christian prayer: "Prayer is the raising of one's mind and heart to God, or the requesting of good things from God."[1] This movement of the mind and heart to God makes Christian prayer a living relationship that is itself a gift of God through Christ. The "heart" of a person is that hidden center in which Christ resides and from where his spirit moves both heart and mind toward God in a relation of love and devotion. As Saint Thérèse of Lisieux puts it, "For me, prayer is a surge of the heart ... it is a cry of recognition and of love, embracing both trial and joy."[2] One responds to trials, one's own or those of others, with prayers of petition or intercession; and to joys or blessings with prayers of adoration, praise and thanksgiving. In all cases, the prayers are the dynamics of a person's relationship with God, where God is both ultimate source and object of the prayers.

Tanaka also makes two comments about Christian prayer in its public forms. First, he questions the appropriateness of public prayers for civic leaders or for teams at athletic events. Does God choose to aid only some political leaders or nations, or choose sides in athletic games? Though I may feel that God must prefer my son's Little League team, or at least Notre Dame football for heaven's sake, certainly God loves and cares for everyone. Perhaps Tanaka's final characterization of Christian prayer is helpful here: "conversational, personal and hopeful." In a public event, one expresses in prayer one's hope, while understanding that God's providence embraces everyone in ways that are larger than one can comprehend.

In the essay by Taitetsu Unno on the Jesus Prayer and Nembutsu, the question of dualism and both the initiative and the consequence of prayer is addressed. Unno points out that according to the Jesus Prayer tradition in Eastern Orthodoxy, the initiative of the prayer is from God, much like the intoning of Nembutsu arising from the Vow of Great Compassion. Here, as in Saint Thérèse's "surge of the heart," the ultimate subject and object of prayer are the same. Unno points out that the consequence of such a Christian prayer is a sense that the world is infused with the presence of God in a way that is similar to finding the Land of Bliss everywhere. Indeed, I would add that this similarity applies to more than just the Jesus Prayer. Saint Teresa of Avila refers to a prayer experience that is not uncommon in mature Christian spirituality "in which is revealed to the soul how all things are in God, and how within himself he contains them all."³

After presenting these similarities between the Jesus Prayer and Nembutsu, Unno raises what he sees as a fundamental difference: the treatment of sin, blind passions, and ignorance. Unno quotes a Christian Orthodox text that calls for the utter rejection of sin and evil, and depicts grace as entering the soul and driving evil outside. Unno then says, "To negate evil, sin, and death means to deny a part of one's reality; to affirm them through transformation means to make one's life complete and whole." The latter approach is, for Unno, key to the spirituality of Shinran and Shin Buddhism. I would like to make two comments here. First, it is unclear as to what Unno is saying about the Shin approach to evil. How can one transform evil into its opposite without evil being "nullified and eradicated"? When the "ice" of one's passions melt into the water of enlightenment, what happens to the passions? Do you have an enlightened person who does evil, acts out his or her passions, and is driven by his or her addictions that remain parts of his or her whole person?

Perhaps what is meant is that the person in the process of enlightenment accepts his or her weakness, foolishness, and lack of virtue as parts of our human condition. But in enlightenment one is free from being bound or trapped by them in ways that define who one is or control one's behavior. If that is the case, then perhaps Shinran is closer to the Christian position than Unno realizes. That is, the soul to which the Christian text refers as the place where grace resides and from where evil is removed is not the whole of the human person. It is the core of one's personhood. When grace dwells within and evil is pushed without, one's personhood, one's identity as a Christian, is formed by the grace of God at one's core, and not the sins of the past or the evil inclinations that still remain a part of one's whole self. It is just that the latter are no longer inordinate; they do not define one's life or habitually bring disorder to one's life and the lives of others.

Rita M. Gross's paper contains a number of important insights about prayer in Buddhism and Christianity. I can only address a few. First, it is encouraging to see Gross's debunking of the view that Christians pray to another being, while Buddhists silently meditate on their breathing. The many ways in which Buddhists pray to relatively existing beings, offer aspirations, and dedicate merit that Gross discusses are certainly proof that this common view is simply incorrect.

It does seem right to me to compare, as Gross does, the inner experience of praying to the deities of Buddhism with the inner experience of Christians praying to saints or angels. Saints are persons born in heaven after death, and angels are "elemental spirits" that populate the universe. One prays for their intercession in seeking help for oneself or others in need, or in overcoming obstacles in the spiritual life. But Gross goes too far in saying that this kind of inner prayer experience is the same as when one prays to God. Again, prayer is relationship in Christianity. One's relationship with God is qualitatively different from one's relationship with other beings — including spiritual ones. This difference can be seen in Christian prayer experiences of God that are of a more nondual nature similar to what Gross refers to as the dissolving of self and other into luminous emptiness. For example, Saint Teresa of Avila speaks of an experience of God: "It is as if in a room there were two large windows through which light streamed in; it enters in different places but it all becomes one."[4] One would never speak this way about the prayer experience of an angel or saint. An experience of union with God as light itself is different from an experience of unity with spiritual beings who reflect that light.

I think that Gross's choice of the serenity prayer as one that Buddhists can find effective and meaningful is itself important. I think everyone comes to a religion with the expectation that it will help change his or her life for the better. In a nontheistic religion, one might be tempted out of a kind of willful enthusiasm to believe that one can change one's life if one has the proper practice, teacher, time, and so on. In a theistic religion, one might be tempted out of a kind of spiritual laziness to give everything to God to change and not really try to change oneself. Christians have often said that humility is the heart of prayer. Perhaps a humble Buddhist has to accept that there are things he or she cannot change. Maybe this is part of Unno's point about transformation. Perhaps a humble Christian needs to accept that there are things he or she *can* change. Here the Christian has much to learn from Buddhists.

In this regard, I have a problem with what Gross says about Buddhists not praying for enlightenment. She says that a deity cannot confer enlightenment because it entails "clearing away confusion and uncovering one's primordial pure and enlightened nature." Then two lines later, Gross says that "Buddhists pray that the *obstacles* to enlightenment might be lessened or destroyed." In Christianity, God does not confer sanctity. God respects human freedom and one is fully involved in the process of spiritual growth by cooperating with grace. This grace is also understood as removing obstacles. Using a metaphor that is also popular in Buddhism, John of the Cross says, "As a fire consumes the tarnish and rust on metal, this consolation [grace] annihilates, empties, and consumes all the affections and imperfect habits the soul contracted throughout its life."[5] Or in words that are not unlike a description of Buddhist insight meditation, the negative psychic states and habits "are brought to light and seen clearly" so that they might be "felt and healed."[6]

Robert Aitken's paper on formal practice is a wealth of examples of Buddhist practices that parallel Christian prayer in some important ways. As one reads this paper, one is reminded of what Gross says about prayer. It is not that God needs our prayer, but that we do. Prayer transforms human experience in both traditions. Aitken presents seven such transformative practices in Buddhist spirituality. Like Unno, he compares Nembutsu to the Jesus Prayer, about which I have commented above. Like Gross, he discusses the extension of merit. Here I am reminded of a daily prayer in my own Focolare spirituality offered each morning. One begins with "Because you are forsaken Jesus, because you are desolate Mary, we offer you this day." Here we understand Jesus as forsaken in humanity, and Mary desolate to find her son in a suffering humankind. So, one offers all of one's day to God for the benefit of others. Later in this prayer, one makes the offering concrete: "I offer you all the prayers, works and suffering of this day." One's day is thus offered to God in a way that changes one's attitude toward others—one lives more for their happiness.

Vows in Buddhism are similar to those in Christianity in that they give form to a person's "determination" or "aspiration" to pursue a higher good. For the Christian this means a renunciation of one's will, a giving of one's freedom in self-emptying for a higher good. Here there is something similar to Buddhism. However, the Christian vow is also taken as an act of devotion to God. Confession in Buddhism and Christianity remind one, as Aitken says, that realization must be sustained, and healing and reconciliation must always be sought when unity is broken. Again, for a Christian this healing and reconciliation includes one's relationship with God. *Dharani, mudras,* and chanting in Buddhism — like certain powerful words, sounds, and body movements in Christianity — create an atmosphere wherein one's senses, mind, and heart are transformed. In this sacred atmosphere, the Christian senses holiness, glimpses something of the divine, and is moved by the inspiration of the Holy Spirit.

In conclusion, I can relate to Aitken's reservations about the "Yes, but..." often heard in conferences on comparative religions. However, I must add my own, "Yes, but I have really learned some valuable things from these papers not only about Buddhist prayer, but prayer in my own tradition." The Buddhist approaches to prayer have given me a new perspective, a greater awareness, and fuller appreciation of the phenomenon of prayerfulness and its potential for spiritual transformation.

Notes

1. Saint John Damascene, *De fide orth.* 3, 24.
2. Saint Thérèse of Lisieux, *Autobiography,* ch. 25.
3. Saint Teresa of Avila, *The Interior Castle,* trans. E. Allison Peers (New York: Doubleday, 1961), 194.
4. Ibid., 215.
5. John of the Cross, *The Dark Night,* II, 6, 5.
6. John of the Cross, *The Living Flame of Love,* I, 21.

A Response to Reflections on Buddhist and Christian Religious Practices

URSULA KING

University of Bristol

I APPRECIATE THE OPPORTUNITY to respond to these essays of personal reflections, comparing Buddhist religious practices with some Christian examples. The different essays are rich in detail, engaging and challenging; they explore new vistas but also point to larger horizons that remain to be explored. Each contribution is so different; each can be read in multiple ways, and further questions can be asked about all of them. Although each contributor has chosen a specific focus, a particular way of interpreting Buddhist religious experience and practice, for me a common thread connects them all. The overarching question, implicitly present even when not explicitly formulated, seems to concern what religious and spiritual practices are really all about.

What is the nature and content, and even more, what is the purpose of religious practice? Can very different practices be compared across different religious traditions? Is it legitimate to compare Buddhist and Christian religious practices, even when they occur in very different contexts and are undergirded by different histories and systems of thought? Is the purpose of all religious practice always spiritual growth and transformation, or is the ultimate goal (if there is such a goal) utterly different and distinct from all such strivings?

There can be no doubt that both external and internal religious practices can be compared at some level, that certain common patterns, shared meanings, and significance, can be discerned in a wide variety of religions. It is these commonalities that phenomenological approaches to the study of religions have extensively explored and classified, but theological, philosophical, and spiritual comparisons are more difficult to delineate. Yet they do exist and have been investigated by many Eastern and Western thinkers. The religious practitioner, who may or may not be a scholar, more often than not remains unaware of the myriad of subtle scholarly distinctions that inhabit a long-trained rational mind. For such a practitioner the strength of spiritual commitment and the practical help in the business of daily living seems to count most when assessing the benefits or otherwise of religious practice. Somehow I find it impossible to capture the ultimate significance of religious practices, whether Buddhist or Christian, within the limits of ordinary language. We always seem to deal with preliminaries, with passing realities rather than abiding truth and ultimate wisdom. Yet we all know of the paradox that there is no other way to the Ultimate than through the Ordinary. It is through the manifold religious practices, however routine and repetitive, that spiritual experience patiently plots its path and weaves its pattern in order to arrive at some eventual destination or be engraced by the gratuitous joy of sudden transformation.

These essays by academic colleagues and friends appealed to my spiritual imagination, and some passages moved me deeply. Their Buddhist insights are enriching and thought-provoking, their references to numerous Christian parallels — whether perceived in meditation, prayer, confession, almsgiving, asceticism, vows, gestures, use of religious texts, or reference to the need for community — sometimes drew my attention to links not seen before, comparisons not encountered earlier. From a Christian perspective I also recognized that some comparisons are only made in passing, so that several comments on Christian religious practices are not as developed as one might expect from an insider's point of view.

All religious traditions, not just Buddhism and Christianity, involve movement, process, and transformation. Each faith tradition, grown over so many centuries and practiced in different societies and cultures by so many different individuals, possesses an ocean of riches that none of us can receive fully. There are major directions and patterns, there are mainstream and marginal practices, but no one would be able to follow them all, nor even want to practice them all, and some may even need to be discarded as obsolete or spiritually unhelpful.

There exists always an excess of spiritual and ritual resources, an abundance of means whereby to find spiritual advance and fulfillment, just as there are a great variety of individual gifts and needs. This is for me the glory and strength of humanity's spiritual heritage that there is so much to select from to be nourished and enlightened by. This is also part of the beauty of interreligious encounter and dialogue that we can help each other on the spiritual path through sharing and mutually illumining parts of our traditions for the benefit of each other.

Several contributors have commented at length on prayer and meditation (Kenneth Tanaka, Taitetsu Unno, Rita M. Gross), highlighting the similarities and differences between Buddhist and Christian approaches to spiritual practices. They also demonstrate that far more parallels can be discovered than previously thought, once one ventures behind existing surface understandings and discards widely held stereotypes, which often contrast these two forms of spiritual practice more than necessary. Tanaka's image of "Megan's Christian prayer" as "conversational, personal, and hopeful" and his emphasis on the petitionary element of Christian prayer do fit many cases of ordinary Christian practice (he judges Christian spirituality as "more accessible to 'ordinary' people"); yet they do not capture the heart of the Christian spiritual tradition, its greatest depth and finest expressions. Christian saints and mystics know of "infused contemplation," nonverbal and imageless forms of prayer, which may well be analogous to certain forms of Buddhist meditation. I therefore see specific forms of prayer and meditation not so much as dualistically opposed to each other than as ultimately convergent forms of the spiritual life. The decisive criterion seems to me to be more related to the differences among the kinds of practitioners than to the differences among the practices themselves. Buddhist religious practices have been much more dominantly shaped by monastics rather than by ordinary lay people, whereas in Christianity there seems to be more of a mixture and balance of lay and monastic spiritual traditions — and depth and superficiality of religious practice can be found in both streams of the tradition. But due to the deeply incarnational approach of Christianity, Christian spiritual practice is much concerned with the spiritual transfiguration of the ordinary, of all of life's experiences in this world, because the divine center and presence in all things transforms everything, so that all ordinary experiences can become the occasion for divine encounter and disclosure. There is a dyadic structure in this pattern, yet not a dualistic one; it is ultimately a unifying process that leads through different means and paths to ultimate oneness and fullness.

Such transformation of the ordinary is certainly at work in the use of the simple but very effective Jesus Prayer of Orthodox Christianity, which Taitetsu Unno and Robert Aitken compare so helpfully with the Nembutsu of the Buddhist Pure Land tradition. The Jesus Prayer belongs to Eastern Christianity, where the affinities to Eastern thought and practices are much stronger than in the Christian traditions of the Latin West. The wider appeal and knowledge of the Jesus Prayer has only come to Christians in the West during the last century. Although it has earlier roots in the Greek Fathers, the Jesus Prayer came into its own in the Byzantine contemplative and ascetical movement of hesychasm, especially as developed by Gregory of Palamas (1296–1359). In this practice, repetitive prayer formulae — especially the Jesus Prayer — are integrated with bodily postures and controlled breathing in order to reach a state of deep inner peace and mystical union. The Jesus Prayer is also seen as "the prayer of the heart." The praying person is seated rather than standing (as was the custom in the East) and is advised to direct the eyes, together with the intellect, toward the middle of the body, to the navel or to the heart, the deep center of unity. Breathing should be carefully controlled in rhythm with the Jesus Prayer or may be coordinated with the beating of the heart itself. Thus the intellect can dispel all thought and search inwardly for the true place of the heart, where inner simplicity, free from all images and discursive thinking, is reached. According to Gregory of Palamas, the prayer of the heart leads eventually to the vision of the divine light, which even in this life can be seen with the eyes of the body. This light is identical to the radiant splendor that surrounded Jesus at his Transfiguration on Mount Tabor, for it is none other than the uncreated energies of the Godhead.

The physical techniques of controlled breathing and concentrated attention upon specific psychosomatic centers of the human body bear similarities to those of Yoga and Sufism. It is possible, though unclear, that the Byzantine hesychasts were influenced by Sufi masters. It is certain, however, that the development of hesychasm helped Eastern Christianity to survive almost four hundred years of Muslim occupation after the fall of Constantinople in 1453. Hesychast spirituality inspired monks and laypeople alike; its simple character and precepts allowed its techniques and prayers to be handed down without schools, literature, or clerical leadership, at a time when Orthodox spirituality no longer enjoyed official support.

During the eighteenth and nineteenth centuries the practice of hesychasm enjoyed a great renaissance throughout Bulgaria, Serbia, and Russia. The publication of the *Philokalia* (1782), an anthology of Orthodox ascetical and mystical writings from the fourth to the fifteenth centuries, and *The Way of the Pilgrim* (1884) made Orthodox spirituality and mysticism, especially the teachings on hesychasm and the Jesus Prayer, widely known to the modern world. Whereas the *Philokalia* consists of texts originally written by and for monks, its eighteenth-century editors intended it for all Christians, and the anonymous *Way of the Pilgrim* is perhaps the work of a devout Russian peasant much inspired by the earlier collection of texts and the hesychast practice of prayer. As a pilgrim traveling through Russia and Siberia he learned the Jesus Prayer from a master who also taught him to read the *Philokalia* with the eyes of the spirit. In turn, his work, *Way of the Pilgrim,* became widely influential and inspired many people in the twentieth century to discover Orthodox spirituality, in many ways so different from that of Western Christianity, and to adopt the practice of the Jesus Prayer. Many could follow on the pilgrim's spiritual path and experience for themselves what he expressed with such intensity when he wrote: "The prayer of the heart provided me with such delight, that I doubted if there were anyone happier than I on earth, or if there could be greater and finer delight in the very kingdom of heaven. Not only did I feel this in my innermost soul, but also all that was around me appeared to me in a delightful form, and all prompted me to love God and to thank him, people, trees, plants, animals, everything was akin to me, on all I found the impress of the name of Jesus Christ."

This passage expresses a holistic and environmentally conscious attitude that hints at the interconnectedness of all beings, and thus resonates with a profound Buddhist insight. Many such resonances and affinities are explored in considerable detail in Robert Aitken's essay on Buddhist and Christian formal practice. Much of this practice is undertaken by the individual, even when together in a group. Aitken mentions in passing the Roman Catholic mass, but much more could be made of the central Christian community rite of celebrating the Eucharist, which not only remembers or makes present Christ's Last Supper, but also brings to mind other invisible communities, such as the communion of saints and that of "all souls" departed. Comparisons between the spiritual group experience of the Buddhist *sangha* and the Christian understanding of spiritual communion and community might perhaps provide a counterbalance to the often too individualistic emphasis on spiritual practice.

However illuminating the comparisons between particular spiritual practices are, the main question remains of how such practices spiritually transform people, a question raised more than once in Rita M. Gross's essay on meditation and prayer. What difference do they make to the people practicing them? Gross has structured much of her discussion around the Christian serenity prayer and some of its Buddhist analogues. Other kinds of Christian prayer would invite comparisons of a different kind. For example, much of Christian prayer is devoted to the adoration of God's very being, greater glory, and intimate presence, or to offering thanks and praise for creation, the giving of life, the sending of Jesus, the utter graciousness of all gifts bestowed on us. These examples would invite other comparisons, as would much of Christian spiritual experience that is expressed in sacred music, from Gregorian chants to the fugues of Bach or the celebrated pieces of Olivier Messiaen or John Tavener. Or what about the spiritual experiences that undergird Christian art and architecture in comparison to those that have shaped the glories of Buddhist art across Eastern continents and cultures? These enshrine not only the experiences of individual practitioners and artists, but express the spiritual vision and experience of an entire culture. Perhaps cultural and communal dimensions are not sufficiently taken into account in Buddhist-Christian dialogue?

Gross describes the theological differences between Buddhism and Christianity as "striking and uncompromising," but considers the forms of spiritual practice as "more similar than different." I wonder, however, whether there is not, between the phenomenological similarities at one end and the theological differences at the other, a middle common ground, a meeting of the ways, where the spiritual transformations achieved by different practitioners on Buddhist or Christian paths are more similar than different?

This leads back to the fundamental question of what spirituality does or, more precisely, what spiritual practices do to people, rather than what those practices are. Do we become more compassionate, loving, and wise? Are we more peaceful, just and kind, equanimous, and generous through following the practices of a particular religious tradition? And do other people perhaps achieve the same result through other means, sometimes even secular ones? The postmodern conditions of our present age present us with such (immensely confusing) possibilities of choice, which also apply to the area of religion and spirituality. While our ancestors in more traditional ages of the past were shaped by the forces of tradition, we are compelled and constrained by the inevitable need for selection. This has opened up immense possibilities of freedom, but it also exercises a quite unforeseen, new form of bondage and a new kind of blinding that makes some people miss the spiritual dimensions of human life altogether. Besides exploring parallels in Buddhist and Christian religious practices, it may be beneficial to investigate on another occasion how these two religious traditions perceive the beginnings of spiritual awakening and what educational and pastoral means they have used to bring about such awakening, which can lead to profound spiritual transformation.

I would like to add here some further reflections on the difference between prayer and meditation. Many people today, both young and old, have some knowledge and experience of these two different modes of centering. It is not my intention, however, to provide a survey here. I only offer a few thoughts of my own. I was surprised to find that the recently published, quite splendid *Oxford Companion to Christian Thought* (eds. Adrian Hastings, Alistair Mason, and Hugh Pyper, Oxford University Press, 2000) has no entry at all on either meditation or contemplation, which it only mentions in passing in the long article on prayer. What does that say about Christianity or, rather, about the late-twentieth-century consciousness of Christian scholars about their own religious tradition?

All religions know different forms of prayer. During the First World War, the German scholar Friedrich Heiler wrote a famous comparative study on prayer, which has recently been republished. But meditation, in contrast to prayer, was far less known in the West until quite recently. How do these two forms of religious expression — prayer and meditation — relate to each other?

Human experiences and formulations of prayer comprise many dimensions, which range from a few personal words to widely known, set prayers used over many generations, from private to public prayers to deeply mystical, wordless prayer experiences of exultation, adoration, supplication, and abandonment. One might almost say that oral prayer moves on into contemplative (using images without words) and meditational (without images or words) exercises.

I think an important distinction is the fact that prayer always seems to be addressed to a personal God (or, in some religions, to several gods) — a very special, great person, almost a "super-person" when seen from an anthropomorphic perspective, but always a personal "Thou" whom we intimately, lovingly or imploringly, speak to. The worship of a personal God is therefore always connected with human prayer, whether traditionally formulated prayers like the "Our Father" in Christianity, spoken by an individual or a congregation, or the Orthodox "Jesus Prayer" which is much more a silent inner prayer. Such deep prayers have been described as the language of the heart, and it is in this deeply personal prayer that our soul breathes and grows in its intimate conversation with God.

All faiths possess a rich heritage of prayers, as can be seen from contemporary anthologies and interfaith services — prayers that human beings have created and uttered in all kinds of different life situations, from the cradle to the grave. There are prayers to address all needs, to plead, to thank, to eat, to travel, to grieve, to celebrate, to adore, for different times of the day and the year, for rites of passage as well as fleeting events — the list is as long as the rich patterns of human life.

Prayer seems to be mostly connected to linguistic expression in words, or even song. Comparing prayer to meditation one might be inclined to emphasize the contrast between such a word-centered religious activity and the silent, wordless inner meditation. But I think it is a mistake to overemphasize such distinction, which, after all, is again an external one. Meditation is for many primarily understood as connected with Eastern religions, especially Buddhism and Hinduism. Meditation has especially arisen within faith contexts that are centered on an impersonal Reality or All, and is thus connected with an illumination or enlightenment understood to be utterly transpersonal. Meditation is closely connected with deep inner concentration and outer withdrawal; meditational techniques bear down on a deep inner center, a transcendent All-ground, although some methods also work with visualizations. But on the whole we associate meditation more with an imageless realization or experience than with anything else. This kind of experience has usually been called "contemplation" in the Christian mystical tradition, whereas the word "meditation" originally meant in Christianity the meditative reflection on specific themes or images, often drawn from the life of Jesus or from other biblical sources.

Comparing prayer and meditation one can say that the intentional direction of prayer is mostly one from inward to outward, from self to other, in that the prayer addresses another Person, the great "Other," so that the self finds a transcendent center for itself, whereas Eastern meditation consists rather of a movement from outward to inward, an effort to reach the immanent center of the self in a deeper dimension within. Thus the direction of prayer and meditation differ; their center is found in a different place and experienced in a different way. But ultimately this difference disappears in that the transcendent and immanent reality touch each other in the depth of being and are ultimately interrelated. One can therefore speak of an interweaving and a continuity between prayer and meditation — the deepest prayer experience of Christian mystics ultimately translates itself into a meditative depth experience of union with the divine ground.

There exists much discussion today regarding the different methods of meditation in East and West. But to speak of meditation is perhaps already a contradiction, because meditation is above all linked to personal practice of concentration and deep inner experience apart from words. And yet such practice requires guidance and training; thus, meditation invites both reflective thinking and practical exercises. We need to learn how to open our mind and heart, how to open ourselves inwardly to be seized by divine grace, or be at peace, be attentive, and be ready to receive the power of the spirit. For Christians, this is connected with the dynamic of divine life, the experience of all — sustaining love — whereas the Buddhist may experience ultimate enlightenment as both emptiness and fullness.

Eastern religions have developed many helpful means for practicing meditation, whether one thinks of bodily postures, breathing exercises, helpful images such as the mandala, or repetition of words in a mantra. All of these have by now become widely familiar and are used by many Western people today. A fine example of interweaving Christian prayers with Buddhist meditation is found in Penelope Eckersley's Nepal notebook *Holding the Silences* (Glastonbury: Abbey Press, 1998). High up in the Himalayan mountains she described her experience: "I closed my eyes to draw myself down into my own stillness, undisturbed by the sights around me and the thoughts to which they give rise." But she also talks of bringing "prayer and meditation out of the limited world of introspection, ethical choices, and self-improvement, into a greater involvement with all that is" (pp. 93 and 89).

I think it is very important to see how closely interrelated prayer and meditation are, and it may be part of the contemporary spiritual renewal to combine the best of the two. In Christian churches people pray a great deal, but there is often not enough meditation. There is far too much emphasis on the spoken word and external action, and yet many people can no longer easily relate to the art of praying. In contemporary culture we are externally overstimulated by words, images, and constant noise, which seem to drown the quiet search of our inner being. Many contemporaries are therefore looking for new wholeness; they need a time and place for quietness and spiritual nourishment. That is why meditation is so popular — a practice many are attracted to, whether they are religious or not.

The Sri Lankan Jesuit Aloysius Pieris has characterized the Christian encounter with Buddhism as "love meets wisdom" (see his book *Love Meets Wisdom: A Christian Experience of Buddhism,* Maryknoll, N.Y.: Orbis Books, 1988). More recently another Sri Lankan priest, Mervyn Fernando, has explored a number of different Buddhist and Christian challenges and parallels, including the interesting comparison of the Buddhist *arhat* and the Christian saint (see his book *In Spirit and in Truth: An Exploration of Buddhist/Christian and East/West Crosscurrents,* Ratmalana: Vishva Lekha Publishers, 2001). Many other parallels and comparisons are discussed in the helpful history of Buddhist-Christian dialogue by Whalen Lai and Michael von Brück (see their *Christianity and Buddhism: A Multi-Cultural History of Their Dialogue,* Maryknoll, N.Y.: Orbis Books, 2001). An ever growing number of high quality, well-informed publications by Buddhist and Christian practitioners and scholars (not to forget the earlier annotated bibliography, *Resources for Buddhist-Christian Encounter,* produced by the SBCS in 1993) help us explore further what comparisons and parallels exist in our respective traditions in the practices and aims of the spiritual life. I celebrate these quite new possibilities of sharing spiritual practices and experiences across our different faith traditions as one of the golden opportunities for discovering new horizons and new spiritual meaning for human life, not only for particular individuals, but for all humanity.

Conclusion

Rita M. Gross

University of Wisconsin – Eau Claire

As noted in the introduction, we had considerably more difficulty finding Buddhists willing to write about the topic of Christian prayer than vice versa. We had trouble finding Buddhists who would agree to contribute an essay, and several who initially agreed later backed out of the project, saying they simply couldn't find anything to say. There is also a marked difference in general between the Christian articles on meditation and the Buddhist articles on prayer. Most Christians report on how they have incorporated Buddhist meditation into their spiritual disciplines, whereas most Buddhists attempt to show that, despite its non-theism, Buddhist practice includes many "prayer-like" utterances.

Why couldn't or didn't Buddhists actually incorporate Christian disciplines of prayer in the same manner as Christians incorporated Buddhist methods of meditation? At first, I thought it might be because some of our Buddhist authors are converts — former Christians — and that experience might make them more reluctant to use Christian prayer personally. But many of our Buddhist authors are *not* converts, and they seemed to have the same reaction.

The answer lies rather, I would argue, in *which type* of Buddhist meditation Christians incorporated into their spiritual disciplines, and *the lack* of a similar type of Christian meditation with which Buddhists could experiment.

Though the terminology may differ, all schools of Buddhist meditation actually teach two types of discipline — *samatha,* or tranquillity, and *vipashyana,* or special insight. *Samatha* meditation involves only calming the mind by placing it on an assigned object of meditation, repeatedly, as necessary, which is usually very frequently, especially for beginning meditators. It also involves letting go of the thoughts that interrupt our ability to stay with the object of meditation, rather than cultivating thoughts in any way. Though the object of meditation could be a figure of the Buddha or another specifically Buddhist object, the most frequently assigned object of meditation is the breath. The breath is assigned for many reasons: noting the breath has a calming effect, the breath indicates life, it is always present and requires no special equipment or place. But, most important, the breath is completely neutral culturally and religiously. As I often say when I am explaining this to non-meditators, it doesn't matter whether you are Christian or Buddhist, religious or non-religious, or subscribe to any other ideology one could think of — we all breathe the same way and depend on breathing in the same way. Buddhists and Christians practicing *samatha* meditation would be doing exactly the same thing. They would place their attention on the breath repeatedly, while not cultivating thoughts — intellectual content — Buddhist, Christian, or mundane.

Vipashyana meditation, by contrast, involves using a calmed mind to investigate the nature of reality, and initially, that involves exploring concepts, though ultimately non-conceptual immersion in reality should happen. It is in *vipashyana,* not *samatha,* meditation that Buddhists explore the teachings of Buddhism, such as the Four Noble Truths or Interdependence. These teachings are not assigned as objects of meditation when one is initially learning *samatha,* though in less introductory, specifically Buddhist contexts, one might be asked to contemplate or ponder these teachings as part of one's daily meditation discipline. Thus, there is a significant different between these two types of meditation: *samatha* involves breaking the hold of distracted conceptuality on our minds and our lives, while *vipashyana* involves using the less distracted mind to explore and ponder more accurate concepts. These two forms of meditation are interdependent, of course, but for teaching purposes, the foundation of *samatha* is always stressed, and the most basic forms of *samatha* involve renouncing, rather than reinforcing, ideology, concepts, and worldview while practicing *samatha,* using the breath as the object of meditation.

Buddhists regard only *vipashyana* as fully Buddhist meditation. *Samatha* meditation is associated with Buddhism because Buddhists have recognized its utility and have taught it for twenty-five hundred years. It is regularly pointed out, however, that Buddha was a master of *samatha* meditation before his enlightenment experience and that *samatha* meditation can be combined with any set of religious teachings when one practices an insight-type meditation in which one is trying to penetrate truth rather than only calming the mind. Buddhists also usually say that, useful and necessary as *samatha* may be, by itself it is insufficient to bring enlightenment. For that one needs not only a calm mind but deep insight into the nature of reality.

Thus, clearly the Christians who use Buddhist meditation are using *samatha* to increase their ability to look deeply into Christian teachings about the nature of reality. They are using a neutral, content-free technique associated with Buddhism to enhance their Christian practice. And Buddhists who teach *samatha* are usually more than happy to lend this assistance. But Christians practicing a "Buddhist" meditation do not usually practice Buddhist *vipashyana*.

As for Buddhists—I know of no comparable neutral, content-free Christian technique of contemplation or meditation that Buddhists could incorporate into their spiritual practice, which explains the difference in the ways which Buddhists and Christians responded to this assignment, in my view. For myself, despite my love of Christian liturgy and my extensive CD collection of Gregorian chant and other Christian liturgical music, I use no Christian forms of prayer or contemplation in my spiritual practice. They all seem to have as a prerequisite a Christian view of the world, and though I mistrust words and concepts to be more than tools or skillful means, Christian words and concepts are foreign to me. I can appreciate them, but I cannot appropriate them into my spiritual discipline.

Spiritual Discipline in Difficult Times

No matter what form of meditation or spiritual discipline is practiced, the expected results are the same. Throughout this volume, Buddhists and Christians have written about each other's spiritual disciplines. It is clear that each author believes spiritual discipline is important, whatever combination of Buddhist and Christian techniques they may use or advocate. Now, in conclusion, it is appropriate to consider some overarching questions about spiritual discipline. First, it would be useful to have a generic definition of spiritual discipline. Second, it would be useful to discuss the relationship between theology or worldview and spiritual discipline. Third, we should ask what difference spiritual discipline makes in peoples' lives. Do people who practice a spiritual discipline regularly and deeply behave differently from people who do not? Finally, of what benefit is spiritual discipline for those living in stressful, difficult times, such as our own.

First, the term "spiritual discipline," which is meant to encompass prayer and meditation, as well as any other disciplines that serve similar purposes. It is difficult to find a truly workable term for these exercises, for some of us aren't fully comfortable with the word "spiritual." What does it mean? It has too many historical connotations of something immaterial that is valued more highly than the physical and material, a thesis many modern Christians and Buddhists would reject. We've had enough religious denigration of the body; furthermore, many spiritual disciplines, including all found in Buddhism, encompass the physical, the body, and materiality within their scope. Nor do the slightly spooky, slightly magical connotations that often inhere in the term "spiritual" sit well with many of us. Spiritual disciplines do not intervene in or set aside mundane realities; they simply take them to a level of which many are not aware because of the busyness and clutter of their minds. Clarity of mind and being able to see deeply are not supernatural, or even unusual, processes. They only seem that way to people unwilling to devote the requisite time and energy to them.

The most important thing about a spiritual discipline is that it involves repetition and regularity, which is why it is often called "practice." Doing it, the activity itself, is far more important than any ideas about it or the expected results. Most experienced practitioners of a spiritual discipline do not expect to "graduate," to a time when the repeated activity will no longer be necessary. We are told to "pray without ceasing," and we are also told to maintain mindfulness at all times in every circumstance. Furthermore, as a practice that is repeated regularly, spiritual discipline is not especially concerned with intellectual speculation or philosophical sophistication. When subjected to intellectual analysis, the content of many spiritual disciplines might seem naïve or simple-minded. This is probably one of the reasons why Western academic studies of religion have failed so miserably to understand what spiritual discipline is or its importance in most religious traditions, including Buddhism and Christianity. Nor is the time spent immersed in spiritual discipline the time for intellectual exploration of one's tradition, no matter how important such exploration may be in other contexts, nor how much the form and contents of a spiritual discipline may derive from the worldview specific to that tradition. Rather, spiritual discipline is an immersion process whereby one opens one's self to ever-deepening insight.

What then is the relationship between spiritual discipline and theology or worldview? Often religious people can recognize each other more readily in spiritual discipline than in theology. For example, Buddhist and Christian worldviews appear to be significantly different on many points, such as the existence of a transcendent creator deity or an immortal personal soul. Nevertheless, a great deal of mutual recognition and even some cross-tradition appropriation of spiritual practice is possible, as the essays in this volume demonstrate. That is because the purpose of spiritual discipline is the same across tradition boundaries, and that similarity of purpose may well be more important than disagreements in worldview, in verbal formulations about the nature of ultimate reality. To me, it is not surprising that when people try to put their deepest experiences and insights into words, they do not come up with the same words, which is one reason why religions are theologically quite different from one another, as well as one reason why the world is an interesting place. However, while I think that some religious ideas make a great deal more sense that others, I personally have never seen theological disagreement to be an ultimate problem or a religiously dangerous situation. I do not lose sleep worrying about the ultimate fate of my friends whose theologies and religious worldviews may be quite different from mine, and I resent people who try to set me straight about my own verbal formulations about truth and reality. (Debate and discussion are another matter entirely.)

Of much greater concern to me is the profundity and depth with which people see into whatever theology they espouse. I do worry about people who profess a great deal of conviction in their religion but do not spend time immersed in contemplation and meditation. I am more worried about the effects of their ideology, unprocessed by spiritual discipline, on the world than about their own well-being, though that is a secondary concern, of course. That is where spiritual discipline enters. People who really have immersed themselves in a spiritual discipline often have much deeper insight into their tradition than those whose understanding is a matter of book learning only. (This statement in no way disparages book learning; it simply points out that it is only one method of delving into religions — a method that has limits if used by itself.)

Those touched by this depth of practice are much less likely to become dangerous to the world and to themselves. People recognize this depth across tradition lines, which is why practical interest in one another's spiritual disciplines and even some experimentation in spiritual disciplines across tradition lines make sense, even for people who are not attracted to theological syncretism.

This function or purpose of spiritual discipline to deepen peoples' insight, to promote and provide spiritual or psychological transformation, is what really interests me about spiritual discipline, about practice, as I have experienced it and observed it. A mind that regularly and repeatedly practices meditation and contemplative prayer is much more flexible and accommodating than one that does not. It is much less rigid and opinionated, much less ideological and self-righteous, much less sure of the correctness of its views, but much more confident about what it is important and what needs to be done. Such a well-practiced mind will be gentle and full of genuine sadness, which is not the same as depression or debilitation, about the state of the world and its suffering. It will not see aggression or revenge as a solution to any of the world's problems and will be filled with non-sentimental compassion for all beings. And all these stances are completely genuine and unfabricated. They do not have to be produced laboriously; they occur spontaneously and constantly. This is the appropriate transformation that emerges slowly and inexorably from consistent spiritual practices. These traits of a well-practiced person do not vary significantly from tradition to tradition. Their presence is much more significant than theological or philosophical views, and the fact that practitioners of spiritual disciplines resemble each other so much across tradition lines re-enforces my claim that theological differences, such as Christian belief in God or Buddhist non-theism, are not so basic or important.

On the other hand, if such appropriate transformation does not occur, then spiritual discipline is not working or is not being pursued properly, and no amount of theological correctness or intellectual pyrotechnics will overcome that flaw. If people claim religion as the basis for their opinionated ideological fixation, their back-and-white dualistic views of the world and of good and evil, then one must question their spiritual disciplines and their methods of practicing such disciplines. Religious conviction is misapplied when people claim that their aggressive, life-threatening or life-taking actions result from their deep religious convictions, no matter what the cause they are supporting or opposing.

Other less aggressive methods more in accord with the fruits of spiritual practice are available to express disagreement with or disapproval of the actions and attitudes of others. It is hard to take seriously those who, claiming a religious basis or motivation for their actions or recommendations, advocate the murder of doctors who perform abortions, issue edits that certain groups of people should be killed whenever possible, or state that a whole religion is demonic. If ever there is a warrant for applying the scriptural verse "By their fruits you shall know them," such religiously motivated hatred and aggression surely merit the judgment implicit in that verse. In these days of fundamentalism and religiously motivated terrorism and warfare, it is important to be able to distinguish genuine religious conviction, transformed and ripened by serious and appropriate spiritual disciplines, from its imitators among those who mistake conviction for aggression and act upon that mistake.

What good is spiritual discipline in times when oppression and injustice are rampant and when vast numbers of people who claim they are religious favor aggression and violence as the way to cope with their pain? One could well wonder whether the world might not be better off without religion when it is used so frequently to justify warfare, aggression, and oppression of those who are different. Religion, misused, has probably caused as much human misery as anything else we encounter.

But what other than genuine spiritual discipline will give us the patience to continue in the face of such discouraging circumstances? What else will give us the patience to remain non-aggressive in the face of so much provocation? What else will enable us to continue to respond with kindness toward those who are aggressive and hateful to us, who would destroy or oppress us if they could? What else can sustain us in the face of pervasive sadness for ourselves and our world? What else can enable us to see so clearly the sacredness of our world and to treasure properly the incredible fragility of our lives?

In these times it is imperative, as it probably has been in all times, for people to talk to each other, within traditions and across tradition lines, about how they find the resilience and confidence to continue to work for peace and justice without aggression, without hostility toward others, simply because peace and justice are lacking. One of the riches of the times in which we live consists in our ability to talk with each other across tradition lines in ways that simply were not possible in the past. For one thing, we barely knew of each other's existence, and, when we did start to learn of each other, often the initial reaction was one of dismissal. Buddhists were seen by Christians as people who wasted time in silent meditation instead of working, and as atheists in a time when atheism and evil were equated. The power of silent transformation present in Christian spiritual disciplines went unrecognized when it occurred in the context of Buddhism. Christians were seen by Buddhists as naïve people who thought that semi-magical incantations and requests to non-existent external deities could help them. Understanding their own praises and petitions to the Buddhas and Bodhisattvas as part of internal spiritual discipline, they assumed that Christians were doing something entirely different in their prayers. But today, after more than a century of exchange, such stereotypes no longer prevail. As the authors of this volume have shown, much can be learned about ourselves and for ourselves from our exchanges with the other. In many ways, we live in difficult, dangerous times. But one thing we can experience to a far greater extent than any generation prior to our own is the ability to appreciate each other's spiritual disciplines and their transformative potential.

Also published by Continuum

BUDDHISTS TALK ABOUT JESUS
CHRISTIANS TALK ABOUT THE BUDDHA

Edited by Rita M. Gross and Terry C. Muck

"This is one of the most intriguing books that I have read for a long time. It has a particular interest because it is one of the few books which gives a free hand to the writers to express their understanding of the key figures of each religion, even if their understanding is not strictly orthodox.... [T]his book contains much thought-provoking material. Though not a large book, it has a great depth, and deserves to be read by anyone who has ever wondered about the relative message of two of the greatest teachers who have ever lived.... As a source material for thought and material for meditation, this book is thoroughly recommended."
— *Pure Land Notes*

"Thought-provoking enough for specialists, these articulate views from informed followers of the 'other' faith are also accessible to general readers. This book is an excellent follow-up to Thich Nhat Hanh's *Living Buddha, Living Christ* and the Dalai Lama's *The Good Heart: A Buddhist Perspective on the Teachings of Jesus.*" — *Library Journal*

"Both Jesus and the Buddha opened up the religious life to marginalized people, stressed the interior life, and inaugurated reformist movements.... Both Jesus and the Buddha had transforming enlightenment experiences of a mystical kind at about age thirty. Both became teachers of a convention-subverting wisdom flowing out of their enlightenment experience.... I tell my students that if Jesus and the Buddha were ever to met, neither would try to convert the other — not because they would regard the task as hopeless, but because they would recognize each other." — Marcus J. Borg